Pistons, Passengers and Payloads

The Evolution of British Commercial Aircraft

ROGER STAKER

KEY Books

HISTORIC COMMERCIAL AIRCRAFT SERIES, VOLUME 24

Front cover image: The DH.91 Albatross is arguably the most beautiful airliner ever built. They transported passengers between Croydon and European cities until the outbreak of war. (Bill Pippin, 1000aircraftphotos.com)

Title page image: The Bristol Brabazon was the mammoth of the skies, but did not proceed beyond the prototype. (Walter van Tilborg, 1000aircraftphotos.com)

Contents page image: The Saro Cloud, a successful amphibian of the 1930s. (Picryl)

Back cover image: The Armstrong Whitworth Argosy pioneered air routes between London and India as well as air mail routes to South Africa. (Bernard Harding collection via Roger Staker)

Acknowledgements
In common with most, if not all aviation history publications, this book is the result of research via the internet and older, sometimes much older, publications. Without photographic content, a work of this nature could not achieve its full potential and I am extremely grateful for the support of those who have made their photographs available. This is very much in the nature of aviation enthusiasts, and their contributions are recognised in the book. Johan Visschedijk (1000AircraftPhotos.com) has been particularly instrumental in pointing me in the right direction and deserves special thanks.

Published by Key Books
An imprint of Key Publishing Ltd
PO Box 100
Stamford
Lincs PE9 1XQ

www.keypublishing.com

The right of Roger Staker to be identified as the author of this book has been asserted in accordance with the Copyright, Designs and Patents Act 1988 Sections 77 and 78.

Typeset by SJmagic DESIGN SERVICES, India.

Contents

Introduction

With less than 11 years between the Wright brothers' first faltering flights and the outbreak of the Great War, it is no surprise that the commercial application of aircraft did not feature highly until hostilities ceased. Paradoxically, the demands of war had contributed greatly to the potential of the aeroplane for civil use.

The technical challenges faced in achieving or maintaining competitive advantage in the skies had ensured the future of aviation. In particular, the technology of aero engines had seen a dramatic evolution. Air-cooled rotary engines of low horsepower, often as low as 80hp (60kW), had given way to liquid-cooled engines with horsepower of 300hp (224kW) or more.

Although a wood framework covered with fabric was still the predominant construction method, aircraft manufacturers had acquired experience and knowledge that meant the structural integrity of their products was much improved.

For the potential use of civilian air travel and the transport of goods to be acceptable and achievable, perhaps the most significant impact of the war was the perception of air transport as being safe and reliable. In fact, it was most definitely not without risk, as events were to prove. There was no air traffic control, no designated air routes or separation of air space for military and civil aircraft and, of course, no radar. Navigation was still achieved by the use of compass and maps, following rivers or roads, all demanding reliance on the trusty Mk 1 eyeball.

Although both airframes and aero engines were much improved, the reliability we now take for granted was still many years away. Nevertheless, the prospect of quick, or relatively quick, transport for business and pleasure, at least for those who could afford it, was tempting. By 1920 there would have been very few people in the United Kingdom who had not witnessed aircraft flying overhead and probably wondered what it would be like to join them. Post-Great War pleasure flights, often in surplus military aircraft such as the Avro 504, gave many their first taste of flight.

As the market/demand for air transport for both passengers and goods grew, so did the demand for larger and more sophisticated aircraft. Inevitably, some manufacturers were better placed than others to meet the commercial challenges involved. There followed both mergers and business failures.

Although early civilian flights were operated by small start-up operators, demand increased and larger airlines were established, with mergers being common. In Great Britain, Imperial Airways was formed in 1924 from a merger of British Marine Air Navigation, Daimler Airways, Handley Page Transport and Instone Air Line.

The early routes, such as the well-patronised London to Paris flights, led over time to much longer multi-day journeys, with stopovers in exotic locations. Trips to Egypt and the pyramids became possible, and even visiting faraway Australia was no longer infeasible.

In 1939, British Overseas Airways Corporation (BOAC), a state-owned airline, was created by merging Imperial Airways and British Airways Ltd. British European Airways (BEA) was founded in 1946 as a division of BOAC.

Hindsight is, of course, a wonderful thing, but an unexpected discovery from the research is the influence that one or two emerging airlines had on aircraft manufacturers' designs. Today we understand the need to talk to potential customers and to take account of their requirements. Unfortunately, it seems clear, if understandable, that because air travel was itself new, airline managers and others with power, including civil servants, did not always grasp the nature and focus of the competition they faced. An example will be found in the design of the Bristol Brabazon, where those with power thought in terms of trans atlantic liners being the competition and felt the need to replicate 'liner' facilities in an aircraft. We now recognise that the competitive advantage was speed. This mindset continued until at least the late 1950s.

It is not unknown for today's travellers to criticise the comfort and facilities delivered by modern jet and turboprop airliners. In the early years of air travel, passengers often sat on wicker or canvas seats without the benefit of seat belts. Few aircraft had toilets and even fewer provided refreshments.

This book describes the piston-engined aircraft that pioneered the aerial transport capability and opportunities we enjoy today. It is a chapter in British aviation history that paved the way for the turboprop and jet engine. Who knows where the future lies?

Chapter 1

Airspeed

Airspeed Ltd was founded in York in 1931. The company's first key directors were Alfred Hessell Tiltman, an experienced aircraft designer who had worked with Geoffrey de Havilland, and Neville Shute Norway, an aeronautical engineer who would become a novelist using his first and second names. Other directors included Alan Cobham, an aeronautical pioneer and Amy Johnson, an aviation pioneer. Financial expertise was provided by Ralph W. E. Beckett, Third Baron Grimthorpe. A. E. Hewitt, a commercial solicitor, also joined the Board.

The first commercial aircraft produced by the new company was the **Airspeed AS.4 Ferry**. This ten-passenger airliner was a three-engine biplane, the design and requirement for which Alan Cobham seems to have been the driving force. The maiden flight took place on 5 April 1932 at Sherburn-in-Elmet aerodrome near York.

The Airspeed AS.4 Ferry standing proudly outside its manufacturer's hangar. (Nico Braas, 1000aircraftphotos.com)

Only four Ferry aircraft were constructed. The first prototype ended up being impressed into RAF service in 1940. Although the second aircraft incurred damage in July 1932, it was repaired and sold to an Indian undertaking, the Himalaya Air Transport and Survey Company, but was destroyed in a hangar fire in 1936. The remaining two aircraft were built for Midland and Scottish Air Ferries Ltd. In September 1934, both aircraft were offered for sale; one of these was not sold, but dismantled. The other was employed by Air Publicity Ltd for pleasure flights and in 1941, it too was pressed into RAF service.

The Ferry's three de Havilland Gipsy engines gave the aircraft a maximum speed of 112mph (180km/h) and a range of 340 miles (550km). It had a wingspan of 55ft (16.76m) and a length of 39 (12.09m).

In 1934, Airspeed introduced the **Airspeed A.6 Envoy**, a twin-engine eight-passenger airliner developed from the company's single-engine monoplane Courier. With a toilet installed, passenger capacity was reduced to six. The aircraft's wingspan was 52ft 4 (15.95m) and the length 34ft 6 (10.52m).

The first prototype had its maiden flight in October 1934. It had been hoped that this aircraft would participate in the MacRobertson Air Race from England to Australia, but it was damaged and unable to fly. The race was won by a de Havilland DH.88 Comet.

The Envoy proved very successful, with 52 being built. Many companies acquired Envoys as airliners, the first UK operator being North Eastern Airways. International interest came from Tata Air Service in India, Ansett Airlines in Australia, Japan Air Transport Company, Czech Airlines and Commercial Air Hire in Spain.

An Airspeed Envoy flies over the *Queen Mary* liner in 1936. (Picryl)

Such was the interest that production licences were negotiated by companies such as Mitsubishi in Japan and Hirtenberger in Austria. In December 1934, an Australian aviator, Charles Ulm, disappeared when flying an Envoy between San Francisco Bay and Honolulu. Although the aircraft had been fitted with additional fuel tanks, it must be assumed that it ran out of fuel before reaching land.

The Envoy's two Armstrong Siddeley Cheetah engines, each delivering 345hp (257kW), gave it a top speed of 210mph (340km/h). It is no surprise that the Envoy found favour with many air forces as well as civil operators. Following the end of World War Two, very few Envoys remained in the UK. The last survivor, disposed of by the RAF, was used for private charter flights until scrapped in 1950.

Early into the war, Airspeed recognised that there would be a need for civil aircraft after the conflict. The successful Envoy had spawned a military version, the Airspeed Oxford, and when hostilities ceased, the company bought back some of these aircraft from the government. Refurbished, they became the **Airspeed AS.65 Consul** and were introduced from 1946.

The Consul had five or, at a squeeze, six seats and the aircraft were fitted with a slightly longer nose for luggage storage. Carpets and leather upholstery were installed. Given the growing post-war demand for civil transport, the Consul was an attractive proposition. A total of 162 were produced by conversion of Oxfords or new build. These were sold to approximately 30 mainly small civil operators in the UK, and more than a dozen overseas airlines.

The successful and popular Airspeed Consul displays its clean lines. (Ed Coates, 1000aircraftphotos.com)

The Armstrong Siddeley Cheetah engines gave the Consul a top speed of 190mph (310km/h) and a range of 900 miles (1,440km).

One of the first post-war new design airliners was the **Airspeed Ambassador**. The initiative for this arose from a study by the Brabazon Committee, established under the leadership of Lord Brabazon in 1942. The Committee's purpose was to consider the future needs of the British Empire for civil airliners following the war. It was no surprise that one recommendation was for a short- to medium-haul aircraft to replace the ubiquitous Douglas DC3. Work on what would become the Ambassador commenced in 1945 and the first of three prototypes made its maiden flight on 10 July 1947. The standard seating layout provided for 47 passengers, and the aircraft could be ordered with or without cabin pressurisation. The aircraft was powered by two Bristol Centaurus 661 engines, each producing 2,625hp (1,957kW), giving a top speed of 312mph (502km/h) and a range of 720 miles (1,160km). Its wingspan was 115ft (35m) and the aircraft's length was 81ft (25m).

The potential of the Ambassador received a huge boost when the newly-established British European Airways (BEA) ordered 20 Ambassadors at a cost of £3 million. These were introduced into service by BEA during 1952, called the 'Elizabethan Class'.

The Airspeed Ambassador's sleek lines are evident in this photo of a British European Airways 'Elizabethan Class' aircraft. (Johan Visschedijk, 1000aircraftphotos.com)

No more sales of Ambassador aircraft took place, meaning that the total built was only 23. There may be several reasons for this. In 1951, Airspeed was taken over by de Havilland Aircraft Company Ltd and the company's new management may have taken a different view on the use of manufacturing resources. In addition, new turboprop airliners were beginning to come to market, such as the Vickers Viscount.

Over time, onward sales of BEA's Ambassadors meant that the type continued in use with smaller UK airlines such as Dan Air, and small numbers went to airlines in Australia and Switzerland.

No account of the Ambassador would be complete without reference to the Munich Air Disaster which took place on 6 February 1958. A BEA flight from Belgrade to Manchester, chartered for Manchester United football team players and officials, as well as members of the national press, had just made a refuelling stop at Munich, where the weather was bad, with heavy snow. After two aborted take-off attempts, the Ambassador again accelerated down the runway but was unable to achieve lift-off speed, due to slush on the runway. In the ensuing crash, 21 of the 44 people on board were killed, with a further two dying later. The accident attracted considerable press coverage.

The acquisition of Airspeed by de Havilland brought to an end the company's involvement in airliner design and manufacture.

Chapter 2

Armstrong Whitworth

Sir W. G. Armstrong Whitworth (Aerial Department) was founded in 1912. During the Great War, the company produced single-engine reconnaissance aircraft for British forces. In 1920, the acquisition of Siddeley-Deasy, a company with an automobile and engine focus, prompted the aircraft interests to be renamed as Sir W. G. Armstrong Whitworth Aircraft Company.

In 1922, Imperial Airways issued a specification for an airliner to serve its Middle Eastern routes. The mainly single-engine aircraft inherited from the companies that had formed the airline needed replacing, so the requirement was quite specific about the range expected and the type of engines to be used. Although the company had not produced an airliner previously, Armstrong Whitworth responded with a proposal for a three-engine biplane airliner that became the **Armstrong Whitworth Argosy**. Imperial Airways liked the proposal and decided that the Argosy could serve its European routes.

The Argosy was constructed with a steel tubing framework supporting a plywood and fabric covering. A wooden floor in the cabin area provided additional bracing. Opening windows and a toilet were impressive features of the aircraft. Baggage was carried in a rear hold, with additional storage in the nose area in front of the pilot. Total passenger capacity was 20.

It was a large aircraft, with a wingspan of 90ft (27.43m) and a length of 64ft 6 (19.66m). The three Armstrong Siddeley Jaguar engines, each of 420hp (310kW) gave the Argosy a maximum speed of 110mph (180km/h) and a range of 405 miles (652km).

The Armstrong Whitworth Argosy served long-haul routes with Imperial Airways. (Neill Bruce, 1000aircraftphotos.com)

The prototype had its first flight on 16 March 1926. The second aircraft flew on 18 June and was delivered to Imperial Airways the following month. On 16 July, Imperial Airways operated its first flight with the Argosy, from London to Paris. The Air Ministry purchased the third machine.

After operating the Argosy successfully for some time, in 1928 Imperial Airways ordered a further four aircraft. The London–Paris service was named the 'Silver Wing' service, and to illustrate its luxury nature, an on-board bar and steward service were provided, albeit at the loss of two seats.

From 1929, Imperial Airways extended its routes to include an air-mail service from London to Karachi. Attempts to extend a regular service to Cape Town were less successful, with climate characteristics impacting reliability.

This Imperial Airways Argosy crashed in Belgium in 1933. (Bernard Harding collection)

Imperial Airways continued to use the Argosy until 1935. Three of the fleet were lost, two of these resulting in no injuries, but on 28 March 1933, an Argosy caught fire over Belgium and the crew of three, together with 12 passengers, were killed. It was thought that a fire in the lavatory was caused by passenger Dr Albert Voss, a dentist from Manchester, who supposedly attempted to commit suicide. He jumped from the plane before it crashed.

In 1927, the Armstrong Whitworth Aircraft Company merged with Vickers and two companies were formed, Vickers Armstrong (generally known simply as Vickers) and Armstrong Whitworth. In 1935, Armstrong Whitworth was purchased by Hawker Aircraft Company.

In 1934, Imperial Airways invited tenders for a large monoplane airliner. It was to be a four-engine aircraft and the designated powerplant was the Armstrong Siddeley Tiger radial engine.

Armstrong Whitworth's response was the **Armstrong Whitworth Ensign**. Discussions between Imperial Airways and Armstrong Whitworth ranged over a variety of options, including the number of engines and the wing configuration. The final Ensign design, with the 'shoulder' location of the wing, was shaped by these discussions. This wing position provided good visibility for passengers and was seen as an important feature for long-distance, and therefore lengthy flights.

Imperial Airways paid for the design and initial construction work in advance. At that time, delivery of the new aircraft was expected in 1936. During 1934, the specification requirements were finalised; the aircraft was to be built in accordance with military structural standards, while there were performance guarantees, including a take-off distance of less than 320 yards (290m) and a cruising speed at 5,000ft (1,500m) of at least 155mph (249km/h).

The Armstrong Whitworth Ensign marked a major technical shift towards monoplanes and away from biplanes. (Picryl)

In May 1935, the airline ordered an additional 11 Ensigns, and in December 1936 a further two were ordered, bringing the total to 14. Unfortunately, political concerns in Europe meant that production priorities in the mid-1930s were directed towards military projects and, in Armstrong Whitworth's case, the Whitley bomber. Additional delays were caused by changes at the request of Imperial Airways, so it was not until 24th January 1938 that the first Ensign took to the air.

The first operational flight, between Croydon and Paris, took place on 24 October 1938. A further three aircraft were delivered by early December. Imperial Airways despatched these three Ensigns to Australia carrying the Christmas mail. None of these managed to reach Australia, due to mechanical problems. Indeed, one of the Ensigns had to return some 2,500 miles (4,000km) with its undercarriage in the lowered position. The undercarriage was hydraulically retractable, and difficulties had been encountered. The main wheels were the largest that had been produced in the UK at that time, measuring 6ft 3 (1.91m).

Imperial Airways returned the five aircraft that had been received to Armstrong Whitworth, which made a number of changes and improvements including the fitting of more powerful Tiger IXC engines.

The Armstrong Whitworth Ensign was a very large aircraft for its time. (Picryl)

Starting in June 1939, the five Ensigns were delivered back to Imperial Airways, together with a sixth aircraft. During the lengthy period they were away, Imperial Airways had changed its plans for Ensign deployment, dropping some of the Far Eastern routes. In 1939, British Overseas Airways Corporation (BOAC) was formed as a state-owned business, through the merger of Imperial Airways with British Airways Ltd.

At the beginning of World War Two, the entire Ensign fleet was initially taken into storage. Each was then painted into camouflage and used on a route to Le Bourget in France. Instead of being pressed into RAF service, they were operated by BOAC under direction from National Air Communications. The war inevitably resulted in the loss of many of the Ensigns, and it appears that only two remained extant following the cessation of hostilities. The final passenger flight was in June 1946 from Cairo to Hurn (Bournemouth) via Marseille. Although both aircraft were offered for sale, there was no interest in them and they were scrapped.

Chapter 3

Avro

Alliott Verdon Roe and his brother Humphrey established A. V. Roe & Company as an aeroplane manufacturing company in 1910. During the Great War, the company, now commonly known as Avro, designed and built both single- and twin-engine aircraft for military service. Many pilots of the early commercial post-war aircraft would have received their flying training on the Avro 504.

In 1920, the RAF needed to replace its ageing Airco D.H.10 Amiens aircraft on the Cairo to Baghdad airmail route, known as the 'Desert Air Route'. It had been established to link Egypt, Palestine and Mesopotamia (now Iraq), which were all under British control following the war.

Avro responded to the requirement with the **Avro 561 Andover**. This was a single-engine biplane with a steel tube fuselage covered with plywood and fabric. The pilot and navigator sat in open cockpits and a passageway led to the cabin, which could accommodate 12 passengers, seated six each side of a central aisle. With a wingspan of 68ft (21m) and a length of 51ft 3in (15.62m), the Andover was quite a large aircraft.

The Avro 561 Andover was a replacement for the Great War bombers that had operated a post-war civilian service. (Ed Coates, (1000aircraftphotos.com)

The maiden flight was on 28 June 1924. Although the RAF had instigated the requirement, the Desert Air Route had been transferred to Imperial Airways, so no Andover ultimately served with the RAF. The aircraft were used for mail, passengers and up to six stretcher cases when deployed as an air ambulance.

Only three type 561 Andovers were built, but a single example of a new version (type 563) was constructed. It had an extra washroom and baggage compartment. This aircraft was used by Imperial Airways for cross-Channel flights during 1925 and was returned to the RAF in 1927. The single Rolls-Royce Condor III engine of 695hp (519kW) gave the Andover a top speed of 110mph (180km/h) and a range of 460 miles (740km).

In 1928, Avro reached an agreement with Fokker to build the successful Fokker FVIIB/3m under licence. Avro called this aircraft the **Avro 618 Ten**. This seems to have been because it could carry a crew of two plus eight passengers.

The 618 Ten appeared in 1929 and the first five aircraft were sold to Australian National Airways, entering service on 1 January 1930 on the Brisbane to Sydney route. However, two of the five aircraft were lost in accidents during 1931. The first of these occurred in the Australian Alps in the south-east of the country. So remote is this area that the wreckage was not discovered until 1958. The second was in Malaysia while a mail flight to the UK was being attempted. The losses resulted in the failure of the airline and the sale of the remaining aircraft.

The Avro 618 Ten was based on a successful Fokker design. (John Hopton, 1000aircraftphotos.com)

In the UK, Imperial Airways purchased two 618 Tens, and Midland and Scottish Air Ferries used one. Other users included Indian National Airways, while there were also some military users. A total of 14 was built.

The 618 Ten had a wingspan of 71ft 3 (21.72m) and a length of 47ft 6 (14.48m). With three Armstrong Siddeley Lynx engines of 240hp (180kW), it had a maximum speed of 115mph (185km/h) and a range of 400 miles (640km).

Avro 618 Tens were still flying into the early 1940s. One owned by BOAC crashed on take-off at Cairo in April 1940 and the last Australian example was used to evacuate people from New Guinea in 1941.

Avro designed and built a scaled-down version of the 618 Ten, called the **Avro 619 Five**. This aircraft accommodated a pilot and four passengers, and the first two were supplied to Wilson Airways in Kenya in 1929. Total production of the 619 Five was only four aircraft, but the remaining two included Avro's demonstrator and the other became a navigational trainer operated by Air Service Training Ltd.

The Avro 619 Five was employed in Africa as well as the United Kingdom. (Johan Visschedijk, 1000aircraftphotos.com)

One of Wilson Airways' aircraft was damaged beyond repair in a forced landing when en route from Salisbury to Broken Hill in Rhodesia. None of the five occupants were seriously injured.

The 619 Five's wingspan was 47ft (14.33m) and its length 35ft 9 (10.90m). It was equipped with three Armstrong Siddeley Genet Major engines of 105hp (78kW). These gave a top speed of 118mph (190km/h) and a range of 400 miles (644km). The last 619 Five was scrapped during World War Two.

Following the success of the Avro 618 Ten, Avro designed a larger aircraft with greater capacity, the **Avro 642 Eighteen**. By 1933, the design stage was complete; the new aircraft would have a welded steel framework for the fuselage and fabric-covered wooden wings. The nose was a wooden structure. The wing was a modification of the 618 Ten's wing but adapted to allow the fitting of Armstrong Siddeley engines.

Midland and Scottish Air Ferries placed an order and by the end of 1933 the aircraft was virtually complete. It was fitted with two Armstrong Siddeley Jaguar VID engines of 450hp (336kW). These gave a maximum speed of 160mph (258km/h) and a range of 600 miles (970km). With a wingspan of 71ft 3 (21.72m) and a length of 54ft 6ins (16.62m), the 642 was Avro's largest aircraft.

This Avro 642 Eighteen's last flight with Commercial Air Hire was a 1936 sightseeing trip around RMS *Queen Mary*. **It became a casualty of World War Two. (Picryl)**

The 642 was handed over to the customer on 6 April 1934 and flown to Castle Bromwich. There it picked up the Prime Minister, Ramsay MacDonald, and Lord Londonderry. They were flown to Speke where a new air service linking Glasgow, London and Belfast was announced.

A second aircraft was ordered by Lord Willingdon, Viceroy of India. This aircraft was delivered in December 1934, but was fitted with four Armstrong Siddeley Lynx IVC engines.

The twin-engine aircraft was sold on in 1935 and deployed on cross-Channel services. After a variety of owners, it eventually went to Australia, but was destroyed by Japanese forces in New Guinea on 21 January 1942. The four-engine example was operated by Indian National Airways, but taken over by the RAF in 1937 and finally dismantled in 1940. Only the two aircraft had been built.

Imperial Airways issued a specification to Avro in 1933, asking for a light airliner to carry four passengers. Performance requirements specified a range of 420 miles (676km) and a cruising speed of 130mph (210km/h). As early as August 1933, Avro's designer Roy Chadwick and his team had produced a design, but Imperial Airways now changed its specification; the aircraft would be required to fly the night mail service between Karachi, Bombay and Colombo.

An amended design was agreed and in April 1934 Imperial Airways placed an order for two aircraft, now called the **Avro 652**. On 7 January 1935, the first aircraft undertook its maiden flight and on 11 March the two Avro 652s were delivered to Imperial Airways at Croydon. They were fitted with two Armstrong Siddeley Cheetah VI engines, each delivering 290hp (220kW). These gave a top speed of 195mph (314km/h) and a range of 787 miles (1,267km). With a wingspan of 56ft 6 (17.22m) and a length of 42ft 3in (12.88m), the 652 was a compact aircraft.

The Avro 652 in civilian guise before being transferred to the Fleet Air Arm. (Bernhard C. F. Klein, 1000aircraftphotos.com)

The Avro 652s operated with Imperial Airways until 1938, when they were sold to Air Service Training Ltd, which used them as navigational trainers. In November 1939, both aircraft were impressed into the RAF, then transferred to the Fleet Air Arm. In March 1942, they were struck off charge.

This may have been the end of the Avro 652 story, but it gave birth to the military Avro Anson, initially known as the Avro 652A. More than 11,000 Ansons were built and served with distinction throughout the world until well into the 1970s. Many were eventually sold to the civilian market and used as company transport.

The Avro Anson, developed from the Avro 652. This one, like many others, retired to civilian life. (Roger Staker)

The outbreak of World War Two in September 1939 signalled a halt to new airliner design and development as military demands consumed resources and focussed initiative on immediate needs.

However, by 1940, BOAC had been formed, and Avro's chief designer, Roy Chadwick, foresaw a need for a long-range transport aircraft. Avro was introducing the Lancaster bomber and identified an opportunity to marry the wings, engines, undercarriage and other 'Lancaster' components to a new fuselage with considerable internal space.

The first prototype of the **Avro York** had its maiden flight on 5th July 1942. This aircraft retained the twin fin and rudder assembly from the Lancaster, but trials indicated that a third, central fin was required for control and directional stability and this became one of the York's best-known characteristics. USAF personnel nicknamed the York as a 'three-fin, four-fan aluminum spam can'.

The Air Ministry did not see a priority for the York, so production was slow. By the end of 1943, only seven aircraft had been built, the third prototype being luxuriously equipped as Winston Churchill's personal transport. This was to change when RAF Transport Command was formed in March 1943 and substantial orders for Yorks were placed. Some of the production aircraft were diverted to BOAC. Peak production took place during 1945, and the last aircraft was produced in April 1948.

An impressive view of the Avro York. (Walter van Tilborg, 1000aircraftphotos.com)

The typical passenger configuration was for 21 passengers seated three abreast in two cabins, although maximum capacity was a crew of five and 56 passengers. There were cloakrooms (for coats), lavatories and a baggage hold. Each cabin had an emergency exit built into the cabin roof.

On 21 February 1944, the first civilian York flight, operated by BOAC, took place from the UK to Cairo via Morocco. Flights to Johannesburg soon followed and for this route, in addition to seating, 12 sleeping berths were fitted.

After the war, BOAC extended the routes served by the York and other airlines purchased the aircraft, including British South American Airways. BOAC withdrew its Yorks from passenger service in October 1952, but retained some for cargo until November 1957. Several smaller airlines purchased aircraft from

BOAC and from British South American Airways. As a result, airlines in Aden, Argentina, Canada, Iran and Lebanon became users. In the UK, Skyways and Dan Air both used Yorks until retiring them in 1964.

The Avro York was a large aircraft with a wingspan of 102ft (31.09m) and the length was 78ft 6ins (23.93m). The four Rolls-Royce Merlin 24 engines, each of 1,280hp (950kW), gave the aircraft a top speed of 298mph (480km/h) and a range of 3,000 miles (4,800km).

The Canadian company Victory Aircraft Ltd acted as a manufacturer of British military aircraft, safe from attack by German bombers. In 1943, the company converted a Lancaster bomber to a civilian transport aircraft for Trans-Canada Airlines, creating the **Avro 691 Lancastrian**.

This Avro Lancastrian flew from England to New Zealand in 1945, but was destroyed in a crash in May 1947 near Cairo. (Picryl)

The success of the project resulted in a further eight Lancasters being similarly converted. After the war, Victory Aircraft was sold to what became Avro Canada.

After the war, demand for civilian transport surged, both for passengers and freight, but there were insufficient civil aircraft to fulfil the need. The conversion of what were now surplus military aircraft helped meet the demand and, beginning in 1945, the delivery of 30 British-built Lancastrians to BOAC commenced. As early as April 1945, a Lancastrian flew from England to New Zealand, averaging 220mph (354km/h) over the three-day 14-hour flight.

The Lancastrian was a Lancaster bomber with armour and armament removed, the gun turrets faired over and new nose and tail sections. The reduction in weight allowed the fitting of two 400-gallon (1,818 litres, 480 US gallons) fuel tanks in the former bomb bay. Space in the aircraft's fuselage was very limited, so it was mainly VIP passengers and freight that were transported. With a crew of four, plus a flight attendant, there would only be room for perhaps nine passengers. A total of 91 were built or converted from Lancasters.

The Lancastrian had a wingspan of 102ft (31m) and a length of 76ft 10ins (23.42m). Its four Rolls-Royce Merlin 24/2 engines, each delivering 1,620hp (1,210kW) provided a top speed of 315mph (507km/h) and its range was up to 4,100 miles (6,600km), depending on payload.

BOAC used the Lancastrians for flights to Australia, and Qantas and Alitalia were also users. Lancastrians proved their worth during the Berlin Airlift when petrol was transported to that city by 15 aircraft making about 5,000 return flights. When London Airport (now Heathrow) opened in 1946, a Lancastrian was the first aircraft to make a scheduled operational flight.

In 1943, Avro considered the recommendations of the Brabazon Committee, which had been established in 1942 to consider the post-war needs for civil aviation. At the time, Avro was working on what would become the Lincoln, a replacement for the Lancaster.

The original idea was to replace the Lincoln bomber fuselage with a new pressurised circular fuselage, but this simple conversion approach was abandoned in favour of a more thoughtful design. Even so, the restrictions imposed by war meant that existing parts, tooling and other resources needed to be used. So it was that the new aircraft, which was to become the **Avro 688 Tudor 1**, retained the Lincoln's wing and the four Rolls-Royce Merlin engines. It also retained the tail-wheel configuration, which was becoming unfashionable in those aircraft that would be its competitors.

Two prototypes were ordered by the Ministry of Supply and built, the first having its maiden flight on 14 June 1945. This was Britain's first airliner with a pressurised cabin. Unfortunately, at this stage the Tudor could only carry 12 passengers, and for an aircraft designed for the North Atlantic route dominated by the Douglas DC4 and Lockheed Constellation, both of which could carry more passengers, this was not a strong selling point.

All the same, the Ministry of Supply ordered 14 Tudors for BOAC and later increased this to 20. The problems did not end there, however. During testing, there were a number of stability issues to be dealt with and larger tailplanes, fin and rudder were fitted. BOAC did not help, requiring no less than 340 modifications before finally rejecting the Tudor in early 1947. Instead, BOAC sought permission to purchase the Lockheed Constellation and Boeing Stratocruiser. Despite this, the Ministry of Supply continued to subsidise the Tudor development and eventually 12 were built, although three were scrapped.

The Avro Tudor 1 had a tortuous and challenging life. (Ed Coates, 1000aircraftphotos.com)

The Tudor 1 had a wingspan of 120ft (35.58m) and a length of 79ft 6ins (24.23m). Its four Rolls-Royce Merlin 100 engines each developed 1,770hp (1,320kW), giving a top speed of 290mph (470km/h).

Avro had considered a larger version of the Tudor (the **Avro 689 Tudor II**) from the outset. With a length increased to 105ft 7ins (32.18m), this was intended to be a 60-seat passenger aircraft and by the end of 1944, BOAC, Qantas and South African Airways had committed to the Tudor II. The prototype flew on 10 March 1946. Changes to the design resulted in some unintended factors, unfortunately, particularly the loss of performance and the inability of the aircraft to be used in hot and high conditions. Qantas and South African Airways cancelled their orders.

The Avro Tudor II was a short-lived and unsuccessful long-distance airliner. (Alamy)

The prototype was destroyed in a crash on 23 August 1947, killing Roy Chadwick. The crash was due to the aileron control circuit being incorrectly assembled. BOAC cancelled its Tudor orders in 1947. In the event, only five Tudor II aircraft were built.

British South American Airways ordered some Tudor I aircraft to be extended by 5ft 9ins (1.75m). These were fitted with Rolls-Royce Merlin engines. By dispensing with the flight engineer's position, they could accommodate 32 passengers, or 28 passengers if the flight engineer position remained. Known as Tudor IV aircraft, the first one flew on 9 April 1947.

During the night of 29–30 January 1948, a Tudor IV disappeared between the Azores and Bermuda. Tudors were temporarily grounded, but were back in action in early December 1948. On 17 January 1949, a second Tudor IV disappeared, this time between Bermuda and Jamaica, and the fleet was again grounded. It was believed that the disasters stemmed from pressurisation problems, so the remaining aircraft were used as unpressurised freight transports. The airline could not continue with fewer airliners, so was taken over by BOAC.

The Tudor's reputation had been so badly damaged that it marked the end of what could have been Britain's first post-war civil aviation triumph.

Chapter 4

Blackburn

Blackburn Aircraft Ltd was founded in 1914 by Robert and Jessy Blackburn, and during the Great War, the company designed and built single and twin-engine military aircraft. Its sole plan to offer a civil passenger aircraft seems to have been the **Blackburn H.S.T. 10**. This was a 12-passenger low-wing monoplane powered by two Napier Rapier VI engines of 365hp (272kW). A crew of two was to be carried, and there was a toilet and baggage space at the rear of the cabin.

It was innovative in design, with a single spar all-metal wing and retractable landing gear. The clean design was expected to give the aircraft a top speed of about 204mph (328km/h). It had a wingspan of 57ft 4 (17.5m) and a length of 42ft (12.8m).

The crew of two shared a control column that could be swung from one side to the other, but each crew member had a separate set of rudder pedals.

Innovation did not guarantee the Blackburn H.S.T. 10 a bright future. (Alamy)

Blackburn's brochure announcing the H.S.T. 10 was dated 1934, so it is safe to assume that the aircraft was built in about 1935 or 1936. It is suggested that it was ordered by British Scandinavian Airways, but that company went into liquidation in 1938.

The Blackburn H.S.T. 10 didn't find a future, except when it was given to Loughborough College as an instructional airframe in 1937. In 1960, Blackburn Aircraft Ltd was absorbed into Hawker Siddeley and the Blackburn name was discontinued in 1963.

Chapter 5

Bristol

The British and Colonial Aeroplane Company was formed in 1910 by Sir George White, who was chairman of the Bristol Tramways and Carriage Company, together with his son and brother. What became simply Bristol Aeroplane Company anticipated the potential of aviation by designing and building some of the most iconic and successful aircraft of the Great War, notably the Bristol Scout and Bristol Fighter, both single-engine military aircraft.

In 1919 and 1920, the company's chief designer, Frank Barnwell, started to plan for a commercial aircraft. The impetus came in 1921 when the British government began to offer subsidies to approved airlines, prompting Bristol's decision to design a single-engine transport aircraft. Understandably, the plan was that this machine would be powered by the Bristol Jupiter engine. However, that engine had not yet been type-approved.

So it was that the first prototype of the **Bristol Type 62 Ten-Seater** undertook its maiden flight on 21st June 1921, with a Napier Lion engine. It had a cabin for nine passengers, the pilot sitting forward in an open cockpit. The second aircraft, designated the **Type 75**, had the Jupiter powerplant, which could be swung forward to allow access to the rear of the engine for maintenance. This aircraft had seating for eight passengers and two crew.

The Bristol Type 75 had innovative features. (Alamy)

The final aircraft, the **Type 79**, was an air ambulance to meet an RAF requirement, Specification 32/22. The wings were given a greater chord and there was accommodation for three stretchers and an attendant, or two stretchers and four seated patients. This aircraft became known as the **Bristol Brandon**.

The Bristol Brandon air ambulance. (Picryl)

In early 1922, the Type 62 was used by Instone Air Line on its London to Paris route. It was eventually transferred to Handley Page Transport Ltd. Instone Air Line had been absorbed into Imperial Airways when the Type 75 was delivered and, because Imperial Airways had a policy of only using multi-engine aircraft for passenger transport, the Type 75 was relegated to a cargo service between London and Cologne. It continued in service until 1926.

The Type 75 had a wingspan of 56ft (17.07m) and a length of 40ft 6 (12.34m). Its Bristol Jupiter IV engine with 425hp (317kW) gave a top speed of 110mph (180km/h) and an endurance of 5 hours 30 minutes.

Although never employed as a commercial aircraft, the **Bristol Type 142** is worthy of mention. It was designed to meet the requirements of Harold Harmsworth (Lord Rothermere), owner of the *Daily Mail* newspaper. In 1934, he challenged Bristol to build the fastest commercial aeroplane in Europe, or possibly the world. He wanted it to carry six passengers and two crew members.

Bristol's chief designer, Frank Barnwell, had the USA the previous year and been impressed by the Lockheed Electra. Subsequent discussions with Lord Rothermere resulted in the design of the Type 142. On 12 April 1935 the aircraft had its maiden flight, and, with a top speed of 307mph (494km/h), it proved to be faster than the RAF's then current fighters!

Lord Rothermere presented the aircraft to the Air Ministry and in September 1935 an order for 150 Type 142 bombers, to become the Bristol Blenheim, was placed.

A Bristol Blenheim Mk 1. (Roger Staker)

In 1942, the UK government established a committee under the chairmanship of Lord Brabazon of Tara to consider and advise on the civil aviation needs of the UK following the conclusion of the war. There had been justifiable concern that the aviation industry was so committed to military demands that the transport needs of the future were being overlooked.

One of the committee's recommendations, Type 1, was for a very large transatlantic airliner. Bristol had considered developing a very large bomber and adjusted its plans to meet the 'Type 1' requirements. These requirements became embodied in Air Ministry Specification 2/44 and Bristol submitted its proposal, resulting in the award of a contract to build two prototypes. Further design work took place and the final shape of the project appeared in November 1944.

The resulting **Bristol Type 167 Brabazon** had its first flight on 4 September 1949. It was, by any standards, a huge aircraft. The internal diameter of the fuselage was 25ft (7.6m), greater than that of a Boeing 747. The wingspan was 230ft (79m) and the length was 177ft (54m). To power this mammoth of the skies, there were eight Bristol Centaurus engines of 2,650hp (1,980kW) each, arranged in pairs driving contra-rotating propellers through combined gearboxes.

A true behemoth of the skies, the Bristol Brabazon enjoyed technical characteristics far ahead of the practical thinking of potential operators. (Walter van Tilborg, 1000aircraftphotos.com)

The Brabazon's internal layout became a source of dialogue and disagreement between the various interested parties, including BOAC. The Brabazon report suggested allowing 200 cubic feet (6 cubic metres) for each passenger, increasing to 270 cubic feet (8 cubic metres) for luxury class passengers. If left to conventional seating arrangements, the Brabazon could have accommodated 300 passengers rather than the planned 60. Other ideas included a cinema, cocktail bar and a lounge.

The eventual accord produced a design with 39 passengers in seven compartments in the front part of the aircraft, 38 upper-deck passengers around tables in groups of four with a pantry and galley, and a further 23 passengers in a rear cinema, the passengers facing aft. With the benefit of hindsight, it is obvious that this was pre-war thinking based on the layout of ocean liners.

Testing of the Brabazon continued, with plans drawn up for a Brabazon Mk II to be powered by Bristol Proteus turboprop engines. However, by 1952, BOAC had lost interest and there were no other interested customers. The project, including the Mk II, was abandoned.

Bristol Aeroplane Company had been focused on the Brabazon project since 1942, but during the war it had developed a plan for a freighter aircraft. The Air Ministry was interested in an aircraft that could carry a 3-ton (907kg) truck, which was a standard British Army vehicle. Interest resulted in Specification 22/44, later revised to C.9/45. In the event, it was too late to participate in the war.

The **Bristol Type 170 Freighter and Wayfarer** owed part of its design to the pre-war Bristol Bombay bomber. It was an all-metal high-winged twin-engine aircraft of sturdy construction. Loading was via clam-shell style doors in the nose. The first flight of the prototype Freighter took place on 2 December 1945.

The second prototype flew on 30 April 1946. This was a 34-seat Wayfarer, which was deployed by Channel Islands Airways, carrying some 10,000 passengers over a six-month period. The third aircraft was a pure freighter with fully operational nose doors. The Bristol 170 attracted interest from around the world and full production commenced.

The managing director of Silver City Airways realised that the aircraft could be equipped to carry cars and passengers from Britain to Europe and to Jersey, thus saving them the long travel times associated with ferries. The company's first flight with a car took place from Lympne in Kent to Le Touquet (France) on 14 July 1948. Silver City Airways was to become a major user of the aircraft and in 1954, each of the company's Freighters averaged 2,970 take-offs and landings.

A Bristol Freighter unloading a car from its clam doors. (Picryl)

In 1953, an extended-length version was introduced known as the Freighter 32. The cargo compartment could be adjusted to carry a variety of payloads with either three cars and 20 passengers, or two large vehicles and 12 passengers. The independent airline Channel Air Bridge began operations from Southend to Calais in 1955.

A Bristol Freighter 32 sporting its extended fuselage. (Johan Visschedijk, 1000aircraftphotos.com)

A total of 214 Bristol Freighters had been built when production ceased in 1958, the last example being delivered to Dan Air in March of that year. These interesting aircraft served a number of air forces across the world as well as civil operators in Europe, Australasia, Asia and Canada.

In 1959, the British government was instrumental in the merger of Bristol Aeroplane Company with other undertakings to form the British Aircraft Corporation.

Chapter 6

Britten-Norman

Britten-Norman was an independent, privately owned aircraft manufacturing and aviation services company, founded in 1954 at Bembridge on the Isle of Wight. John Britten and Desmond Norman had both trained with de Havilland, and in the 1950s they developed crop-spraying equipment, which they deployed on modified de Havilland Tiger Moths for a contract in the Sudan.

An analysis of the aviation market had indicated an unsatisfied need for a rugged commuter aircraft capable of operating from rough landing strips, and the company was formed to create just such an aircraft. The result was the **Britten-Norman BN-2 Islander**.

The first flight of the Islander took place on 13 June 1965, powered by two Rolls-Royce/Continental engines. These engines were replaced by Lycoming 0-540-E4C5 engines providing greater power. Early production took place at the company's headquarters in Bembridge, but demand for the Islander eventually outstripped the ability to deliver, so a contract was placed with a Romanian company, Intreprinderea de Reparații Material Aeronautic. More than 500 Islanders were assembled in Romania, and in August 1969, the first Romanian-built Islander took to the air.

A very successful light transport, the Britten-Norman Islander was designed and built on the Isle of Wight, hence its name. (Roland Hottelet, 1000aircraftphotos.com)

The Islander had a passenger capacity of nine. Its wingspan was 49ft (14.94m) and its length 35ft 7¾ins (10.86m). The Lycoming engines, generating 260hp (190kW) each, gave the aircraft a maximum speed of 170mph (274km/h) and a range of 869 miles (1,398km).

Britten-Norman went into receivership in October 1971, but the company was acquired by the Fairey Aviation Group in August of the following year. Development of the Islander and of the military version, the Defender, continued. Approximately 1,280 Islander/Defender aircraft were built and are in operation throughout the world.

A larger variant of the Islander format was developed in the late 1960s. This was the **Britten-Norman Trislander**. Capable of seating up to 18 passengers and with the ability to undertake short take-off and landing operations, the Trislander was a logical addition to the basic Islander format.

The first flight took place on 11 September 1970, and Trislanders began operations with Aurigny Air Services Ltd of Guernsey during July 1971. Of the 73 completed Trislanders built, Aurigny operated 16 at one point. Production ceased in 1982. As with the Islander that preceded it, the Trislander had found customers throughout much of the world.

The Britten-Norman Trislander was the Islander's big brother. (Rudy Mantel, 1000Aircraftphotos.com)

The Trislander had a wingspan of 53ft (16.15m) and its length was 49ft 3 (15.01m). The three Lycoming engines each produced 260hp (190kW), giving the Trislander a maximum speed of 180mph (290km/h) and a range of 1,000 miles (1,600km).

Chapter 7

De Havilland

Geoffrey de Havilland joined the Army Balloon Factory in 1910. During the period to 1913 he worked on designs for single engine reconnaissance, fighter, and bomber aircraft, moving to Airco (the Aircraft Manufacturing Company Ltd) in 1914. When the Great War broke out, he became a designer in what was now called the Royal Aircraft Factory.

The post-war slump in demand for aircraft resulted in Airco's acquisition by the Birmingham Small Arms Company, but with help Geoffrey de Havilland formed his own company, de Havilland Aircraft Company Ltd in 1920.

Before he left Airco, Geoffrey de Havilland had designed an eight-passenger transport aircraft, which became known as the **de Havilland DH.18**. Although the first prototype had been built by Airco, and indeed was in service with Aircraft Transport and Travel Ltd before being wrecked in a forced landing, the additional aircraft under construction were transferred to the newly formed de Havilland company when Airco went into liquidation.

The de Havilland DH.18 was involved in the world's first mid-air collision of civilian transport aircraft. (Picryl)

In the event, a total of six DH.18 aircraft were built, three being used by Instone Air Line. One of these was transferred to Daimler Airway for its Croydon to Paris route. Only two days after the service commenced, this aircraft collided with a Farman Goliath over northern France. As its name implies, the Goliath was a larger, heavier aircraft and a wing and the tail of the DH.18 were severed. It crashed immediately, killing the pilot and a boy steward who was on board. The Goliath crashed a few minutes later, killing all five on board. This was the first mid-air collision involving civilian aircraft.

The DH.18 was retired from commercial service in 1923.

The 450hp (340kW) Napier Lion engine gave the aircraft a top speed of 125mph (201km/h) and a range of 400 miles (640km). It had a wingspan of 51ft 3ins (15.62m) and a length of 39ft (11.89m).

Experience acquired from the DH.18 resulted in design work starting on new passenger aircraft, but the plans for a ten-passenger monoplane (DH.29) plus a replacement for the DH.18 with a more economical engine (DH.32) were abandoned following consultation with potential users. Instead, a nine-passenger biplane was designed, the de Havilland DH.34. It could accommodate two pilots.

The aircraft was built with a wooden framework and plywood covering. The single Napier Lion engine generated 450hp (340kW), giving a top speed of 128mph (206km/h) and a range of 317 miles (510km). It had a wingspan of 51ft 4 (15.65m) and a length of 39ft (11.89m).

The first flight took place on 26 March 1922 and the aircraft was delivered to Daimler Airway on 31 March, entering service on the Croydon to Paris route on 2 April. Daimler operated six DH.34 aircraft, with Instone Air Line using a further four. A single example was built for the Soviet airline Dobrolyot.

The de Havilland DH.34 operated on European routes, but its safety record was severely compromised. (Johan Visschedijk, 1000aircraftphotos.com)

The DH.34's excellent safety record was shattered in November 1923 when one crashed near Leighton Buzzard. The aircraft was operating on the London to Birmingham route when it got into difficulties and then nose-dived at high speed into the ground. Six of the 12 DH.34 aircraft built were lost in accidents, some of them fatal.

The scale of the de Havilland DH.34 is evident from this photo. (Johan Visschedijk, 1000aircraftphotos.com)

On 1 April 1924, Imperial Airways was formed and absorbed Daimler and Instone, with six remaining DH.34s being transferred to the new airline. In March 1926 all of these were retired.

Geoffrey de Havilland's awareness of the changing nature of aviation since the Great War resulted in recognition that war-surplus aircraft would need to be replaced. De Havilland designed a four-passenger aircraft using experience gained from the DH.9 of 1917, and the result was the **de Havilland DH.50**. It had its first flight on 30 July 1923, and during the remainder of that year and into 1924, the DH.50 achieved success in air races, reliability trials and long-distance flights.

Genuine interest in the DH.50 saw a total of 38 aircraft being built. Of these, only 17 were actually built by de Havilland, the remainder being constructed under licence in Australia, Belgium and Czechoslovakia. In Australia, operators included Qantas, Western Australian Airways and Holdens Air Transport. A DH.50 was the first type of aircraft used by the Flying Doctor Service.

The de Havilland DH.50 was at the birth of the Australian Flying Doctor Service. (Picryl)

In Belgium, Sabena used the DH.50 on routes in the Belgian Congo, with the last one being withdrawn in 1937. By 1942, all surviving DH.50 aircraft had been retired.

The DH.50 had a wingspan of 42ft 9 (13.03m) and its length was 29ft 9 (9.07m). With a Siddeley Puma 230hp (170kW) engine, it had a top speed of 109mph (175km/h) and a range of 380 miles (610km).

The growing stature of Imperial Airways resulted in the company taking over responsibility for the airmail service between Cairo and Baghdad from the RAF. The RAF had been using DH.10 Amiens bombers of Great War vintage and these were rapidly becoming obsolete, so Imperial needed a suitable aircraft for this route.

De Havilland designed a three-engine biplane with capacity for seven passengers in addition to the mail cargo. To cope with the climatic challenges of the region, the fuselage was a steel tube frame covered with plywood mounted inside the cabin and baggage compartment. Two pilots sat in an open cockpit and the cabin had accommodation for a wireless operator in addition to the passengers. This aircraft was the **de Havilland DH.66 Hercules**.

The first Hercules had its maiden flight on 30 September 1926, Imperial Airways having already ordered five aircraft several months before. This is almost certainly because the company had committed to a five-year contract for the airmail service and needed the Hercules to deliver it. The prototype and the second aircraft flew to Cairo in December and the first commercial service began on 7 January 1927. With the inauguration of a Cairo to Delhi service in 1929, Imperial Airways ordered another Hercules, bringing its total complement to seven.

A de Havilland DH.66 Hercules, a true long-distance airliner. (Dan Schumaker, 1000aircraftphotos.com)

West Australian Airways ordered four DH.66 aircraft, which were built in 1929 and could accommodate 14 passengers.

On 8 September 1929, there was a fatal crash on landing at Jask in Iran. Because the Hercules was out of production, Imperial Airways purchased a replacement from West Australian Airways. In 1931, an airmail service between Croydon and Melbourne, via Karachi, was inaugurated. Imperial purchased another Hercules from Western Australian and when this was delivered to Karachi, it operated the first mail delivery from Australia to the United Kingdom.

The DH.66 Hercules of Imperial Airways, damaged beyond repair in a forced landing in Indonesia in April 1931. (Picryl)

Imperial Airways withdrew the Hercules from service by 1935, but a DH.66 was used by Stephens Aviation in New Guinea until 1942, when it was destroyed by enemy action.

The Hercules had a wingspan of 79ft 6 (24.23m) and a length of 55ft 6ins (16.92m). The three Bristol Jupiter VI engines, each of 420hp (310kW), gave it a top speed of 128mph (206km/h).

Building on de Havilland's success in designing and building light aircraft, the company developed a small and economical light passenger aircraft called the **de Havilland DH.83 Fox Moth**. It had a passenger capacity of three or four in the enclosed cabin, the pilot sitting in an open cockpit on top of the fuselage. In this manner, it was not unlike the earlier DH.50.

Design took place late in 1931 and the aircraft that emerged had a wood-framed fuselage with plywood covering; the wings, tailplane, fin and rudder were identical to those of the DH.82A Tiger Moth, which was also being built at that time. The Fox Moth's wings could be folded for storage.

The first example undertook its maiden flight on 29 January 1932. The prototype was sent to Canada, where sufficient interest was generated for production of seven aircraft to begin, with that figure greatly increased following the end of World War Two. In total, 153 Fox Moths were constructed, with the bulk of these in England; two were built in Australia and 53 in Canada.

The de Havilland DH.83 Fox Moth proved itself in Australia and beyond. (Picryl)

The Australian experience is significant. A Fox Moth started operating between Launceston on Tasmania and Whitemark on Flinders Island, a 108-mile (174km) route over the Bass Strait. It established what was to become Australian National Airways and later, Qantas. Fox Moths replaced the ageing DH.50 aircraft with the Australian Flying Doctor Service.

Other users included Air Travel (New Zealand) Ltd, Wardair Canada, Tata Airlines (India) and Aeroput (Yugoslavia). A number of small British airlines operated Fox Moths including Hillman's Airways, Midland and Scottish Air Ferries, Northern and Scottish Airways and Provincial Airways. In practice most had been retired from operational service by the time that World War Two began.

The Fox Moth with the de Havilland Gipsy III engine of 120hp (89kW) had a top speed of 106mph (171km/h) and a range of 425 miles (684km). Its wingspan was 30ft 10.7ins (9.41m) and the length 25ft 9 (7.85m).

Hillman Airways' positive experience with the Fox Moth encouraged this airline to ask de Havilland to produce a twin-engine version. Utilising a simple plywood box fuselage and some components from the Fox Moth, the resulting aircraft had its first flight on 12 November 1932. This was the **de Havilland DH.84 Dragon**.

With a single pilot and capacity for up to 10 passengers, or six with their luggage, the Dragon was to prove an attractive proposition for small airlines. Following the prototype, the next four aircraft were delivered to Hillman's and in April 1933, the company began a London to Paris service for six passengers. Fuel consumption was 13 gallons (49 litres, 15.6 US gallons) per hour.

The attraction of the Dragon meant that airlines across the world were soon operators of the aircraft. It was used by airlines in Australia, Brazil, Canada, Czechoslovakia, India, France, Egypt, Ireland, Kenya, New Zealand, Portugal and South Africa as well as the United Kingdom. Although mainly small regional airlines used it, Qantas in Australia and Aer Lingus were larger concerns of note.

An early de Havilland Dragon landing in Perth, Western Australia, in 1987. (Roger Staker)

Late in 1933, a change was made to the undercarriage through the provision of a streamlined fairing. The result was an increase in the top speed by 5mph (8km/h), an increase in payload of 250lb (113kg) and a range addition of 85 miles (137km).

A variety of accidents occurred, however. together with a particularly bizarre incident. On 21 February 1935, two American sisters (Jane and Elizabeth Du Bois) purchased all the seats on the Hillman's Airways flight from Stapleford (Essex) to Paris. When they turned up alone for their flight, they claimed that their companions had been unable to fly. There were therefore only three people on the Dragon, the pilot and the two sisters. Over the English Channel, the pilot became aware that he was now alone in the aircraft. The bodies of the two sisters were found at Upminster, East London. There was speculation that their suicides resulted from the deaths of RAF pilots a few days earlier, with whom they had been romantically linked.

Production of the Dragon in the UK ceased after 115 aircraft had been built, but in Sydney, production continued for the Royal Australian Air Force, with a further 87 being constructed. A total of 202 Dragons was therefore built.

The Dragon was powered by two de Havilland Gipsy Major I engines of 130hp (97kW) each. The maximum speed was 128mph (206km/h) and the range 460 miles (740km). Its wingspan was 47 (14.43m) and its length was 34ft 6 (10.52m).

A special Dragon was built for Amy Johnson and her husband Jim Mollison, both pioneering aviators with long-distance achievements to their credit. Their plan was to fly non-stop from New York to Baghdad. After a series of mishaps with the aircraft, however, the attempt was abandoned. Even so, the fuel tanks and engines were installed in a second Dragon and the new owners of the aircraft, James Ayling and Leonard Reid, took off from Wasaga Beach, Ontario, to fly to Baghdad. Throttle problems curtailed the flight and it was obliged to land at Heston, near London. Still, it had flown for 30 hours 55 minutes, marking the first non-stop flight between Canada and Great Britain.

An inter-governmental agreement in 1933 established an air mail service between constituents of the British Empire, comprising the United Kingdom, India, Malaya, the Straits Settlements and Australia. On 22 September 1933, Australia invited tenders for delivery of air services over legs of the Singapore–Australia route, with the aircraft continuing south to land in Tasmania.

To facilitate Qantas Airways' securing the Singapore to Brisbane route, the company pre-empted the tender process by placing an order with de Havilland for an aircraft, which would become the **de Havilland DH.86 Express**. Qantas assumed that ownership of an aircraft capable of providing the service would greatly help to secure the tender. It was a key requirement that the prototype should fly by late January 1934.

The Qantas order was soon followed by another from Holyman's Airways, based in Launceston, Tasmania. This concern wished to make flights across the Bass Strait segment between mainland Australia and Tasmania.

The DH.86 was based on the successful but relatively basic Dragon, but was larger, with four engines and much more attention to streamlining focused on the fuselage, the use of fairings for the wing struts and particularly the undercarriage. Unlike the Dragon's square-cut wings, the DH.86's wings were tapered. De Havilland selected its most powerful engine, the 200hp (149kW) Gipsy Six, for the new aircraft.

For long-range services, de Havilland proposed a single pilot and a wireless operator, together with accommodation for ten passengers. For shorter routes, passenger numbers were increased to 12. The prototype first flew on 14 January 1934.

The single-pilot configuration was immediately rejected by Qantas because of the dangers of pilot fatigue, so the DH.86 nose was redesigned for two pilots. Although the first prototype was rebuilt for two pilots, three other aircraft were built and delivered with a single-pilot layout. One of these entered service with Holyman's in October 1934 and at that time it was the world's fastest British-built passenger aircraft. Thirty-two were built in total.

The de Havilland DH.86 Express; lessons were learned but too late. (Bernard Harding Collection)

The next 20 aircraft were fitted with pneumatic landing gear, a metal rudder and changes to the windshield. These were designated as the DH.86A. After a series of fatal crashes, modifications to the fins were implemented in 1936, with these aircraft being designated DH.86B.

In addition to Qantas and Holyman's, New Zealand's Union Airways and Britain's Railway Air Services were users of the DH.86. There were three fatal crashes in Australia and others in Europe.

The Aeroplane and Armament Experimental Establishment tested the DH.86 design in 1936 as a result of the accidents. Only some years later was the report made available to the airline operators, and it seems that the failure of the DH.86 and its variants stemmed from the haste with which the aircraft had been designed and flown (only four months). This was the result of pressure from the Australian airlines anxious to win airmail contracts. The aircraft was large for its engine power and was lightly built in order to provide adequate performance. The conclusion was that under standard operating conditions, the aircraft was safe, but could quickly go out of control in some situations.

When production ceased in 1937, a total of 62 DH.86 aircraft had been built. Although a few survived the war, the last commercial aircraft was destroyed by fire in 1958.

The DH.86A had a top speed of 166mph (267km/h) and a service ceiling of 17,400ft (5,300m) with a range of 760 miles (1,220km). Fuel of 1,145 imperial gallons (5,205 litres/1,375 US gallons) was carried in the undercarriage fairings. The wingspan was 64ft 6in (19.66m) and the length 46ft 1¼in (14.05m).

During late 1933, de Havilland designers worked on a successor to the successful Dragon, one that would be faster and more comfortable, with accommodation for eight passengers. In appearance and in terms of some features, the aircraft that emerged was a scaled-down version of the DH.86 Express. Its wings were tapered and the undercarriage was contained within a streamlined fairing.

This new design was known as the **de Havilland DH.89 Dragon Rapide**. It would prove to be an extremely successful small airliner.

The prototype's maiden flight took place on 17 April 1934. During the following month, this aircraft underwent airworthiness trials, at one point reaching a speed of 175mph (282km/h). The nose of the Dragon Rapide started to buckle, however, and in consequence all Dragon Rapides were limited to 160mph (260km/h).

By the end of 1934, full-scale production of the Dragon Rapide was under way. Hillman Airways was the first company to take delivery, in July 1934, and from August, Railway Air Services operated services linking London, the north of England, Scotland and Northern Ireland using a fleet of Dragon Rapides. Isle of Man Air Services was another early operator, with air links to Blackpool, Manchester and Liverpool.

Late in 1935, a batch of aircraft was shipped to Canada, where minor modifications were made to meet local conditions. Quebec Airways and Canadian Airways were early operators.

The de Havilland DH.89 Dragon Rapide was a great success, both as a civil airliner and also in its military form. (Roger Staker)

Upon the outbreak of World War Two, UK-based aircraft were requisitioned for military purposes, some being used for civilian internal flights until April 1940 as directed by National Air Communications. A progressive return to civil aviation was allowed when this was deemed to be in the national interest.

Production of the Dragon Rapide ended in November 1941, but de Havilland continued production of a military version called the Dominie. Ultimately, 728 Dragon Rapide and Dominie aircraft were built, and there were few countries where the type had not been deployed in either a civil or military role.

The Dragon Rapide had a wingspan of 48ft (14.63m) and a length of 34ft 6 (10.52m). The twin de Haviland Gipsy 6 engines generated 200hp (150kW) each. The maximum speed was 157mph (253km/h) and the range 556 miles (895km).

In 1935, the Air Ministry issued Specification 36/35 for an aircraft to perform a transatlantic mail service. De Havilland responded with a four-engine design of a unique balsa and plywood 'sandwich' construction. This material would later become famous for its use in the wartime Mosquito.

The **de Havilland DH.91 Albatross** was arguably the most beautiful four-engine airliner ever made. The air-cooled engines were mounted in such a way as to maximise the streamlining and minimise drag. A 22-passenger version differed from the original mail plane concept in having more windows and slotted flaps rather than split flaps.

Two prototypes, both mail planes, were constructed, the first flight taking place on 20 May 1937. Imperial Airways operated both prototypes, and a further five passenger aircraft were ordered and delivered during 1938 and 1939. These were operated on routes from Croydon to Paris, Zurich and Brussels.

The beautiful lines of the de Havilland DH.91 Albatross are clearly evident. (Bill Pippin, 1000aircraftphotos.com)

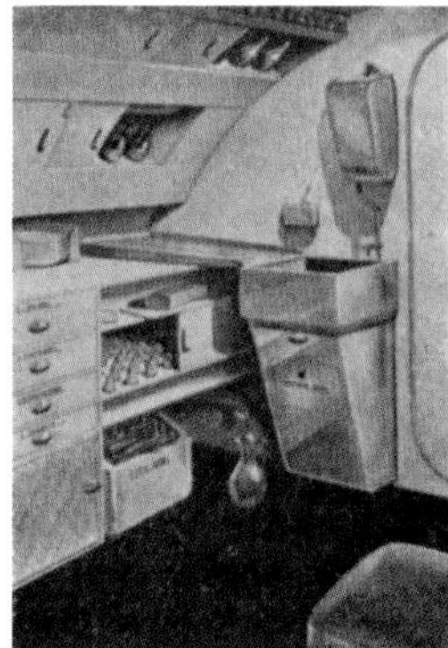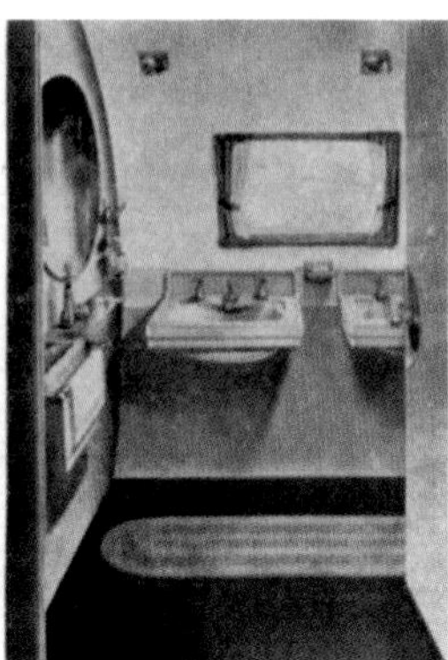

Not only was the Albatross's design innovative, but the interior concept was a perfect accompaniment. (Picryl)

When war broke out, the two mail planes were requestioned by the RAF and used for flights between Prestwick and Reykjavik. Both, however, succumbed to landing accidents at Reykjavik. The five-passenger aircraft were operated by Imperial Airways, and then BOAC, on flights from Bristol to Lisbon and Shannon. Following the loss of one Albatross by enemy action and two through accidents, the remaining aircraft were scrapped in September 1943. This was prompted by the fact that its plywood wings were deteriorating and had caused one of the accidents.

Changing times; the modern monoplane Albatross behind the venerable but ageing Handley Page HP.42 Heracles biplane. (Bernard Harding collection)

The Albatross had a wingspan of 105ft (32.01m) and a length of 71ft 7ins (21.83m). The four de Havilland Gipsy Twelve engines, each of 415hp (309kW), gave the aircraft a top speed of 225mph (362km/h) and a range of 1,070 miles (1,720km).

In 1936, Ronald Eric Bishop became de Havilland's chief designer. He had worked for the company since 1921, when he joined as an apprentice at the age of 18. His first new aircraft project was the **de Havilland DH.95 Flamingo**.

This was de Havilland's first all-metal stressed-skin aircraft, only the control surfaces being fabric covered. Power was provided by two Bristol Perseus XIIIC engines, each of 890hp (660kW). The crew of two pilots and a radio operator sat in the forward cockpit. The cabin could accommodate up to 17 passengers, although 12 was the practical limit on longer flights.

The prototype had its first flight on 22 December 1938 and on 30 June 1939, it was granted a certificate of airworthiness. An initial production line of 20 Flamingos was planned, with Jersey Airways the first airline to place orders, but only the prototype seems to have been operational before the outbreak of war. The other aircraft ordered were requisitioned by the Air Ministry.

As can be seen from this photograph, the de Havilland Flamingo's civilian life was short-lived. (Picryl)

In 1940, BOAC ordered eight Flamingos with Bristol Perseus XVI engines of 930hp (690kW) and these were moved to Cairo to operate in the Middle East. The aircraft were not popular with BOAC. There were three accidents, one of which was fatal, and in 1943, the remaining aircraft were returned to the United Kingdom and stored, but were ultimately scrapped in 1950.

Conversely, Winston Churchill liked the Flamingo for short- or medium-distance journeys. His long-distance favourite was the Avro York, and it may be that the similar high-wing layout was attractive to him because of the view it allowed.

With the Perseus engines, the Flamingo had a top speed of 243mph (391km/h) and a range of 1,345 miles (2,165km). The wingspan was 70ft (21.34m) and the length 51ft 7in (15.72m).

After the war ended, de Havilland, along with other manufacturers, considered how to meet the growing demand for air transport. The Brabazon Committee had identified as one of its recommendations (number VB) the need for a short-haul feeder aircraft for British airlines to replace the Dragon Rapide.

A serious competitive consideration was the inevitable surplus of former military transport aircraft following the war, particularly the large numbers of Douglas DC3/Dakotas.

The result of de Havilland's development was to become the **de Havilland DH.104 Dove** and it would prove to be a great success. The Dove was an all-metal aircraft with seating for eight to

11 passengers and was designed to allow the operator to convert the seating arrangements to suit their requirements. The lavatory and luggage compartments could be removed to increase seating for short flights.

Attention was also paid to the simplification of maintenance, with interchangeable components and built-in facilities to ease engine removal, for example. Although designed for a pilot and radio operator as a standard, the Dove could be quickly equipped with dual controls for another pilot. The cockpit had a transparent Perspex roof in addition to good-sized windows to maximise pilot visibility and light.

The prototype first flew on 25 September 1945 and the Dove entered service with Central African Airways in December 1946. By the time production finally ceased in 1967, a total of 544 Doves had been built, including 130 military versions. During the type's long production life, a number of variants emerged. The first version was powered by two de Havilland Gipsy Queen engines of 330hp (250kW), but the last version had de Havilland 400hp (300kW) Gipsy Queen 70 Mk 3 engines. Some conversions in the USA even had turboprop engines.

This de Havilland Dove was the personal transport of the late King Hussein of Jordan. It is being escorted by the Royal Jordanian Air Force aerobatics team. (Roger Staker)

The Dove was sold to numerous airlines throughout the world from 1946. More than 50 were sold to operators in the USA, while in Australia, several regional airlines deployed the Dove, as did the Australian Royal Flying Doctor Service. Other airlines of note included SABENA of Belgium, Union of Burma Airways (later Myanmar National Airlines), West African Airways Corporation, Indian National Airways, East African Airways Corporation, South African Airways, BOAC, Silver City Airways and Jugoslovenski Aero-Transport. There were many others, not to mention military users, which covered much of the world.

A few Doves remained in use with small commercial operators beyond 2010, but they have largely been retired or scrapped.

The de Havilland Dove had international appeal. (Picryl)

When equipped with the 400hp (300kW) de Havilland Gipsy Queen 70 Mk 3 engines, the de Havilland Dove had a top speed of 230mph (370km/h) and a range of 880 miles (1,420km) when carrying a payload of 1,398 (1,634kg), and allowing for a holding pattern of 45 minutes with a 5 per cent reserve. The wingspan was 57ft (17.37m) and the length was 39ft 3in (11.96m).

A logical development of the Dove was to enhance its appeal by increasing its size and therefore its passenger capacity. A stretched aircraft with two more engines would provide a robust airliner for regional and commuter routes where rugged simplicity would make for a reliable service. Given the nature of the airports, or, more likely, airfields from which the aircraft would operate, a fixed undercarriage was selected.

The **de Havilland DH.114 Heron** had its first flight on 10 May 1950. By increasing the length to 48 6in (14.78m) and the wingspan to 71ft 6in (21.79m), the passenger capacity of the Heron was 14 to 17. Four de Havilland Gipsy Queen 30 engines were installed, each producing 250hp (190kW); these gave the Heron a cruising speed of 160mph (257km/h).

British European Airways used the prototype on Scottish routes and deemed it a success, prompting de Havilland to begin production. New Zealand Airways was the first major user, but was to find deficiencies with the Heron, considering the aircraft underpowered and discovering that the fixed undercarriage limited performance. Perhaps more seriously, the wing spars were cracking due to the weight of the engines and the rough landings to which the Heron was subjected at many grass airfields that were common in the country. Although New Zealand Airways endeavoured to deal with the problem by replacing the alloy spars with steel, this further limited performance and the company disposed of its Herons in 1957.

De Havilland recognised the issue and, from the 52nd aircraft, the Heron had a retractable undercarriage, becoming the Heron Series 2. Cruising speed was increased to 183mph (295km/h) and fuel consumption was reduced. A total of 149 Herons (Series 1 and 2) had been built when construction ceased in 1963.

This de Havilland Heron is a Series 2 version with the retractable undercarriage. (Bryan Gibbins, 1000aircraftphotos. com)

Despite the limitations of the Heron Series 1, it was a generally well-liked aircraft and it served both civil and military users throughout much of the world. In addition to the United Kingdom, Herons were used by civil operators in no less than 32 countries.

De Havilland Aircraft Company was acquired by Hawker Siddeley in 1960, but continued to operate as a separate company until 1963. It will always be remembered for the world's first commercial jet airliner, the de Havilland Comet.

Chapter 8

Handley Page

andley Page Ltd was founded by Frederick Handley Page (later to become Sir Frederick Handley Page) in 1909. It was the first established British aircraft company and was at the forefront during the Great War, building large multi-engine bombers, including the twin-engine Handley Page 0/100 and 0/400 aircraft and the four-engine Handley Page V/1500.

Thus, experienced in the design and development of large aircraft, the company recognised the potential for civil transport, developing a prototype based on its wartime 0/400 bomber. Known as the Handley Page W.8, this aircraft first flew in December 1919. It had a cabin with capacity for 15 passengers, but the Air Ministry insisted on a number of changes. These included reducing passenger capacity to 12, repositioning the fuel tanks and the installation of less powerful Rolls-Royce Eagle engines, although these were to prove more economical than the original Napier Lion engines. The Handley Page W.8 series was the first airliner to be designed with an on-board lavatory.

Three of the revised aircraft, the **Handley Page W.8b**, were ordered by the Air Ministry in 1921 for use by Handley Page Transport (later Imperial Airways). These were operated on services to Paris and Brussels. In 1924, Belgium's national airline SABENA purchased one, and a further three were built under licence in Belgium.

The Handley Page W.8b was the first in a long line of commercial aircraft from the company. (Picryl)

The Handley Page W.8 cabin shows just how far developments had come. (Picryl)

Further developments would take place. To minimise the risks of engine failure, the **Handley Page W.8e** was equipped with a Rolls-Royce Eagle IX engine of 360hp (270kW) and two Siddeley Puma engines of 240hp (180kW) each between the wings. SABENA acquired the first aircraft and had an additional ten built in Belgium.

More variants emerged; the **Handley Page W.8f Hamilton** and W.8g were three-engine developments that involved changes to the tailplane and rudder arrangements, eventually dispensing with the nose engine and fitting two Rolls-Royce F XIIA engines, each of 480hp (360kW).

The Handley Page W.8f Hamilton. (Picryl)

The **Handley Page W.9a Hampstead** was a three-engine version fitted with Armstrong Siddeley Jaguar IV engines of 385hp (290kW) each. On the London to Paris route, Imperial Airways managed a record flight of 86 minutes.

The Handley Page W.9a Hampstead attracting the attention of the press. (Picryl)

The final version of the W series was the **Handley Page W.10**. This twin-engine aircraft with 450hp (340kW) Napier Lion engines was built for Imperial Airways, with four being completed.

The last of the W line, the Handley Page W.10. (Neill Bruce, 1000aircraftphotos.com)

In total, 25 W Series airliners were constructed and had advanced the future of air transport.

In 1928, Imperial Airways issued a specification of requirements for airliners to operate over long-distance routes. The **Handley Page HP.45** and the externally identical **Handley Page HP.42** were designed to meet these requirements. The HP.42 was intended for shorter European routes, sacrificing fuel load for passenger numbers, while the HP.45 went on to fly passengers to exotic places such as Egypt, with its pyramids.

The construction was metal, except for fabric covering of the wings and rear fuselage. The HP.45 was powered by four Bristol Jupiter XFBM supercharged engines each developing 555hp (414kW). The HP.42 had four Bristol Jupiter XIF engines of 490hp (365kW) each.

The first aircraft flew on 14 November 1930 and in June 1931 carried its first fare-paying passengers to Paris. All the aircraft were given names, each beginning with the letter H and chosen for historical or mythological significance. The first aircraft to fly was *Hannibal*.

Handley Page HP.42 *Hannibal*. This aircraft went missing over the Gulf of Oman on 1 March 1940, with the loss of four crew and four passengers. (Bernhard C. F. Klein, 1000aircraftphotos.com)

The aircraft had a top speed of 120mph (190km/h) and a range of 500 miles (800km). The wingspan was 130ft (40m) and the length 92ft 2in (28.09m). The HP.42 could carry 24 passengers and 14.2 cubic metres of luggage.

Hannibal in flight. (Bernhard C. F. Klein, 1000aircraftphotos.com)

Both types had served well when they were withdrawn from civilian service on 1 September 1939. There had been no major accidents or fatalities in almost a decade of service.

By early 1940, the surviving aircraft (three HP.42s and three HP.45s) were pressed into RAF service as transport aircraft. None of them survived beyond 1940, except *Helena*, which was scrapped in 1941. It was a sad end to an amazing line of aircraft.

Handley Page's experience in the design and construction of large multi-engine aircraft continued during World War Two, so it was well-placed to provide aircraft for the rapidly growing demands of commercial aviation when hostilities ceased. Like Avro, Handley Page had a four-engine bomber, the Halifax, which with relatively minor changes could deliver an interim solution until newly designed aircraft were available.

To provide aircraft for BOAC, ten Halifax C Mk VIII transport aircraft were converted to 10-seat airliners by Short Bros and Harland. These were designated as the **Handley Page HP.70 Halton**. They were powered by four Bristol Hercules 100 engines, each of 1,675hp (1,249kW), providing a top speed of about 280mph (450km/h). The Halton had a wingspan of 104ft 2in (31.75m) and a length of 71ft 7in (21.82m).

There were many Halifax bombers surplus to requirements after the war, and a large number of civil conversions were performed by a variety of contractors. Whilst not all would have been fully up to the Halton standard, as many as 80 such conversions are believed to have been undertaken.

A Handley Page Halton showing the luggage pannier under the fuselage. (Picryl)

During the Berlin airlift of 1948/49, 41 civil Halton or Halifax aircraft were used, nine of which were lost during the operation. The last civilian-operated aircraft was retired in 1952. In addition to BOAC, British operators of the Halton included Bond Air Services and Westminster Airways. With a range approaching 2,400 miles (3,860km), the Halton was a suitable aircraft for services to Cairo and beyond.

In mid-1943, the Air Council, which included the body responsible for running the Royal Air Force together with the Air Ministry, considered the future requirements for RAF transport aircraft and the need for a civil airliner for the immediate post-war years, seeing as the RAF's existing Handley Page Halifax freighter/transport aircraft would have a limited capacity and lifespan.

Handley Page made proposals for both a military and a civil response. In December 1944, the Air Ministry placed an order for the civil airliner set out in Specification 15/43. This included pressurised accommodation for up to either 34 first class passengers or 50 tourist class passengers. An internal decision was made by Handley Page to merge some projects and to prioritise the military transport. This aligned with Specification C.3/44, which sought a multi-purpose military transport aircraft.

However, it became apparent that development of a civil aircraft would be less challenging than a military transport, so it was decided that the civil airliner should be the first to fly. Names were allocated to the planned aircraft, with the military transport to be the Handley Page Hastings, while the civil airliner would be the Handley Page HP.67 Hermes.

The Hermes prototype took off for its maiden flight on 2 December 1945. It did not go well; the aircraft crashed almost immediately after take-off, killing Handley Page's chief test pilot, together with the chief test observer. The Hermes was completely destroyed by fire. The cause was attributed to overbalancing of the elevators, which generated severe longitudinal instability and loss of control.

The inevitable delay to work on the Hermes meant that priority shifted to the Hastings, development of which doubtless benefited from the catastrophe that had occurred with the Hermes. However, it also provided an opportunity to revise the Hermes project. The length of the aircraft was increased and the second prototype emerged as the Handley Page HP.74 Hermes II. Like its unfortunate predecessor, it had a traditional tail-wheel undercarriage. The first flight took place on 2 September 1947.

BOAC had placed orders for 25 Hermes airliners in early 1947, and these were to be the definitive **Handley Page HP.81 Hermes IV** aircraft, equipped with a tricycle undercarriage. Although Handley Page had considered fitting turboprop engines, the aircraft were powered by four Bristol Hercules radial engines, each of 2,020hp (1,510kW). A certificate of airworthiness was issued on 4 September 1948.

The Handley Page Hermes IV, a short-lived long-haul airliner. (Philo Lund, 1000aircraftphotos.com)

Introduced to initial operations in early September 1948, the Hermes was considered by BOAC as being too heavy. Handley Page recognised that this resulted in part from the incorporation of Hastings components, as well as some ad hoc changes that had been made during flight trials. As a result, modifications were made, which included lighter-weight floor members.

It was therefore not until 6 August 1950 that the Hermes finally entered service. It replaced the Avro York on the service from London to Accra (Ghana) via Tripoli, Kano (Nigeria) and Lagos. Later in 1950, services to Kenya and South Africa began. Use of the Hermes by BOAC did not last long; in 1952, the feet was replaced by Canadair Argonauts, although the type was briefly reprieved in July 1954 due to the grounding of the de Havilland Comets, only to be finally retired by BOAC in December 1954. Overseas airline operators of the Hermes included Bahamas Airways, Kuwait Airways and Middle East Airlines. Surplus aircraft were sold to independent airlines such as Skyways, Britavia and Airwork. The final operational flight, with Air Links Ltd, was on 13 December 1964. A total of 27 piston-engine Hermes were built, together with a further two aircraft powered by turboprops.

The Hermes IV carried a flight crew of five, together with cabin crew. Passenger capacity was 40 to 82, varying in accordance with the nature of the service. The maximum speed was 357mph (575km/h) and the range between 3,145 to 3,550 miles (5,060 to 5,715km) depending on payload. Its wingspan was 113ft (34m) and the length was 96ft 10 (29.51m).

In 1947, Handley Page secured the assets of Miles Aircraft Ltd. That company had designed a four-engine airliner with seating for 20 passengers, in line with the recommendations of the Brabazon Committee for post-war commercial aircraft. There was possibly also a target to produce a successor to the de Havilland 86 Express. Three prototypes had been built and flown before the Miles company was forced to declare itself bankrupt.

The aircraft, called the Miles Marathon, was the company's first all-metal aircraft and also its first four-engine design. Although it was well-designed and complied with the requirements of the International Civil Aviation Organisation, there had been little, if any, engagement with potential purchasers and operators.

During the design stages, there were internal disagreements about the parameters of the new aircraft, particularly focusing on the size/weight of the proposed machine and the number and type of engines. What emerged was a high-wing four-engine monoplane powered by de Havilland Gipsy Queen engines of 340hp (250kW) each. The Air Ministry issued Specification 18/44 based on the design, but this did not, however, give Miles the authority to proceed. The concept received the approval of the Brabazon Committee, but the Specification was issued for competitive tendering in May 1944. Bids from companies such as Percival and Armstrong Whitworth were received, as well as Miles, and it was not until October 1944 that Miles was selected to produce the aircraft. Even so, the Air Ministry rules prohibited the company from contacting potential users, which means that their requirements could not be considered. These may well have been public sector rules, but they made little commercial sense.

Although the design had basically been finalised by April 1945, a variety of public bodies became involved, each trying to have their specific, and sometimes contradictory, requirements incorporated. The inevitable disputes and, from Miles Aircraft's position, trying to understand who had the overall authority, resulted in delays and the waste of resources all round.

Nevertheless, on 19 May 1946, the first prototype had its maiden flight. Flight testing went well, with the aircraft being praised for its handling by the test pilots. Although Miles had been instructed to proceed with the Marathon, this did not constitute a production contract from government sources. It was not before the second prototype was flying and the third was at an advanced stage of construction that contract negotiations were completed. Even then, the contract was for 50 aircraft, when Miles had expected 100. It was too late for Miles Aircraft and the company went bankrupt in late 1947.

Handley Page acquired the majority of the assets and committed to producing the Marathon, now called the **Handley Page HPR 1 Marathon**. The order for 50 aircraft was split between British European Airways (BEA), with 30 allocated, and the remaining 20 for BOAC. These had already been earmarked by BOAC for re-sale to other airlines.

On 10 May 1948, one of the prototypes crashed during trials at Boscombe Down, a disaster attributed to pilot error.

Even during Miles Aircraft's control of the Marathon's development, consideration had been given to the replacement of the Gipsy Queen engines with two turboprop units, and on 19 May 1947, the Air Ministry issued Specification 15/46 for a turboprop-powered version of the Marathon. The Specification called for use of the Armstrong Siddeley Mamba engines, but the Rolls-Royce Dart was seen as an alternative. A single Mamba-powered prototype was built and flew in July 1949. This aircraft became significant when it was re-engined with Alvis Leonides engines, playing a part in the development of the next Handley Page airliner, the Herald.

Handley Page Marathon, designed by Miles. (David J. Gauthier, 1000aircraftphotos.com)

The first of 40 production Marathons left its Woodley, Reading, base on 14 January 1950, flying on a sales tour that embraced Australia and New Zealand. Although this Marathon was later painted in BEA colours, the airline did not consider it as a viable replacement for its de Havilland Dragon Rapides, and although some Marathons were ordered by BEA, none were actually accepted.

West African Airways Corporation purchased six, but these were replaced in 1954 by de Havilland Herons. The final three production aircraft were supplied to the Union of Burma Airways and operated for several years. In 1955, Derby Aviation, a predecessor of British Midland Airways, acquired three Marathons, which were operated on routes within the UK and to the Channel Islands until retired at the end of 1960.

The Ministry of Supply ended up with a large number of Marathons, probably as many as 30. They were used by the RAF for navigational training but were not well received in this role. By 1962, all Marathons had been scrapped.

The four de Havilland Gipsy Queen 70-3 engines of 340hp (250kW) each gave the Marathon a top speed of 233mph (375km/h) and a range of 935 miles (1,505km). The wingspan was 65ft (19.81m) and its length was 52ft 1.6ins (15.89m).

Building on the experience with the Marathon, and with the target of developing a replacement for the ubiquitous Douglas DC-3, Handley Page began work on a new design in the mid-1950s. Like the Marathon, the design was a high-wing airliner. The company consulted operators of the DC-3 and concluded that the new aircraft should be powered by conventional piston engines, rather than making the leap to turboprop propulsion. The familiarity of ground staff with this mode and the associated ease of maintenance were probably considerations.

Handley Page preferred a four-engine design, so the new aircraft would be powered by Alvis Leonides Major radial engines, each of 870hp (650kW). The resulting aircraft was the **Handley Page HPR3 Herald**.

Designed to carry a crew of two and up to 44 passengers in a pressurised cabin, the Herald could also be adapted for transport of cargo, with the high wing and nose-wheel undercarriage providing easy access via large doors at the front and rear of the cabin. The aircraft was fitted with large flaps to provide short take-off and landing characteristics.

Sales activity had secured an encouraging level of interest from prospective purchasers. Interest from Queensland Airlines, Australian National Airlines and a Colombian airline had produced orders for 29 Heralds prior to the prototype's first flight, which took place on 25 August 1955. Handley Page had good reason to expect a commercial success.

The original Handley Page Herald, a good design but with the wrong engines. (Alamy)

Unfortunately, the market and the competition were moving towards turboprop propulsion rather than piston engines. Only three months later, the Fokker F.27 Friendship took to the air, powered by two Rolls-Royce Dart turboprops. Worse still, both Queensland Airlines and Australian National Airlines cancelled their orders in favour of the Dart-powered Vickers Viscount.

Handley Page made the only sensible decision available and that was to relaunch the Herald as a Dart-powered airliner. The second HPR3 prototype was re-engined with turboprops and went on to achieve some success, but valuable time had been lost and it was not until 1961 that the new aircraft went into service.

UK government pressure on the aircraft industry to merge into large organisations meant that by the late 1960s, there were only two major companies, Hawker Siddeley and the British Aircraft Corporation. Handley Page resisted this impetus but could not compete, and in March 1970 the company went into voluntary liquidation. So ended 61 years of aircraft production under the Handley Page name.

Chapter 9

Miles

In 1928, Charles Powis and Jack Phillips established a company called Phillips & Powis Aircraft (Reading) Ltd, based at Woodley Aerodrome near Reading. In 1932, Frederick George Miles met Charles Powis and agreed to design a light aircraft to be called the Miles Hawk, which Phillips & Powis sold with success. In 1935, Rolls-Royce became a major shareholder in what was now a public company. Miles became chairman and managing director, while his brother George became the test pilot and managed the aero engine department.

In 1941 Rolls-Royce lost interest in the company; Frederick Miles bought control and renamed it Miles Aircraft Ltd in 1943.

Following success with the Miles Hawk and other light aircraft, Miles designed a twin-engine light transport aircraft in 1936, calling it the **Miles M.8 Peregrine**. It provided accommodation for a crew of two and six passengers. Powered by two de Havilland Gipsy Six II engines, each of 205hp (153kW), the Peregrine had a top speed of 188mph (303km/h). It also had a retractable undercarriage.

The prototype first flew on 12 September 1936. It had been entered in an air race from Portsmouth to Johannesburg known as the Schlesinger Race, but was too late to participate as the race itself took place in September. Of the 14 entrants, only nine aircraft actually took part.

The Miles M.8 Peregrine was completed too late to take part in the Schlesinger Race. (Dan Schumaker, 1000aircraftphotos.com)

Late in 1937, the first Peregrine was dismantled and a second aircraft was built with more powerful Menasco Buccaneer BS6 engines of 290hp (216kW) each. This went to the Royal Aircraft Establishment and was used as a flying laboratory for boundary layer trials.

The first Peregrine had a wingspan of 46ft (14.02m) and a length of 32ft (9.56m).

Towards the end of World War Two, the company developed a light freighter design for both military and civilian use. Intended as an affordable and rugged aircraft that could operate in conditions that were less than ideal, it would be relatively low-powered and suited to short-range operations.

Work on what would become the **Miles M.57 Aerovan** began in earnest in early 1944. The aircraft was built with plastic-bonded plywood, together with some spruce and metal components. The tricycle undercarriage and high-mounted tail assembly, coupled with the deep-sided fuselage and clam doors at the rear, provided ease of loading and justified the Aerovan name. The aircraft was powered by two Blackburn Cirrus Major III engines of 150hp (112kW) each.

The prototype undertook its first flight on 26 January 1945, and it soon became apparent that the Aerovan had capabilities well above its modest size and power. It could accommodate a family car loaded through the rear doors and payloads of one tonne (2,205lbs, 1,000kg) could be carried.

The prototype Miles Aerovan showing its four square windows. Later aircraft had five windows in a slightly longer fuselage. (Dan Schumaker, 1000aircraftphotos.com)

Understandably, Miles believed that the Aerovan's characteristics would be of real benefit to the war effort, and provided the Air Ministry with data from the trials. Far from securing support and interest, however, the company was firmly rebuked for daring to build the aircraft without approval and all further work was stopped on Air Ministry orders.

When hostilities ceased, development continued. Interest from potential civilian customers was immediate and, in fact, Miles was overwhelmed by orders, so it was not until 1946 that production commenced in any quantity. The production aircraft differed from the prototype primarily in having an 18in (46cm) longer fuselage.

The main operators of the Aerovan were commercial companies. The aircraft were employed in a wide variety of roles, including transport of livestock across the English Channel and as flying removal vehicles. However, the majority were employed on passenger and freight services. In addition to the UK, civilian users were located in Angola, Belgium, France, Iraq, Italy, Kenya, the Netherlands, New Zealand, Spain, Switzerland and Turkey. A total of 48 Aerovans were built, with minor changes over four variants.

One of the UK users was Meridian Air Maps, an aerial survey company based at Shoreham in West Sussex. It had the misfortune to suffer two fatal accidents with its Aerovans, the first of which was on 29 April 1957, when Aerovan G-AISF took off from Ringway (Manchester International). It failed to gain height and bounced along the runway until overturning when it hit the metal perimeter fence. The two passengers and pilot were killed, and it was a sad end to pilot Jean Lennox-Bird, the first woman to receive RAF Wings. Later that year, Aerovan G-AJKP crashed near Oldbury in Worcestershire while carrying out survey work. The pilot was the sole occupant and was killed. According to an eyewitness, the starboard wing separated in flight and 'fluttered' down.

The ill-fated Miles Aerovan G-AJKP photographed at Shoreham in mid-1957, a few months before its fatal crash. (Roger Staker)

The Miles Aerovan (Mks 2,3 and 4) had a wingspan of 50ft (15m) and a length of 36ft (11m). The maximum speed was 127mph (204km/h) and it had a range of 400 miles (640km).

After World War Two ended, state control over aircraft production was greatly eased and the Miles company was keen to benefit from this relaxation. One of its successful designs had been the single-engine Miles Messenger, and the company based its design for a new twin-engine aircraft on that concept. What emerged was the **Miles M.65 Gemini**, a four-seat light transport aircraft.

Much of its construction was from plywood with plastic bonding, while power was provided by two Blackburn Cirrus Minor II engines of 100hp (75kW) each. These provided the Gemini with a top speed of 150mph (240km/h) and a range of 520 miles (840km).

The prototype had its first flight on 26 October 1945 and sales demonstrations were launched straightaway. Such was its popularity that within the first year 130 Geminis had been sold. Not surprisingly, many of these were acquired by private individuals and commercial organisations for their own business transport requirements. Among these companies was the Shell petroleum company, one of whose senior executives was Sir Douglas Bader, RAF flying ace.

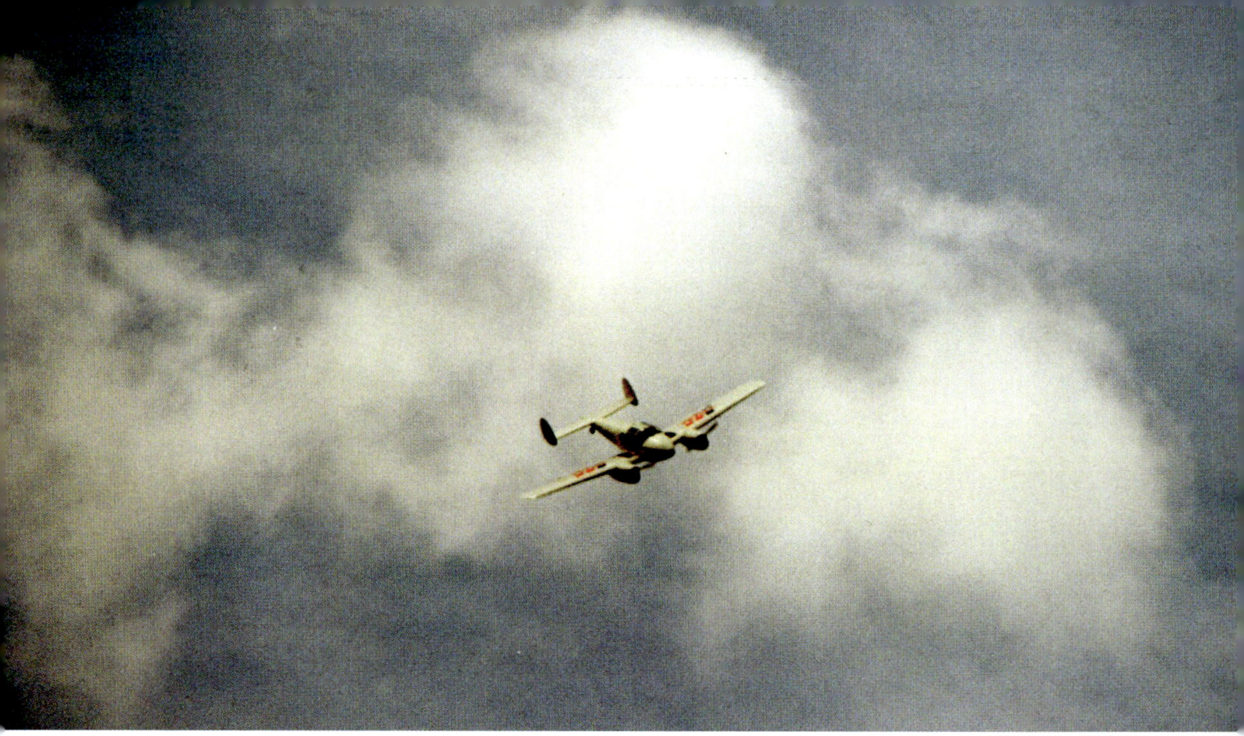

The Miles Gemini in its element. (Roger Staker)

The clean lines of the Miles Gemini displayed on the ground. (Picryl)

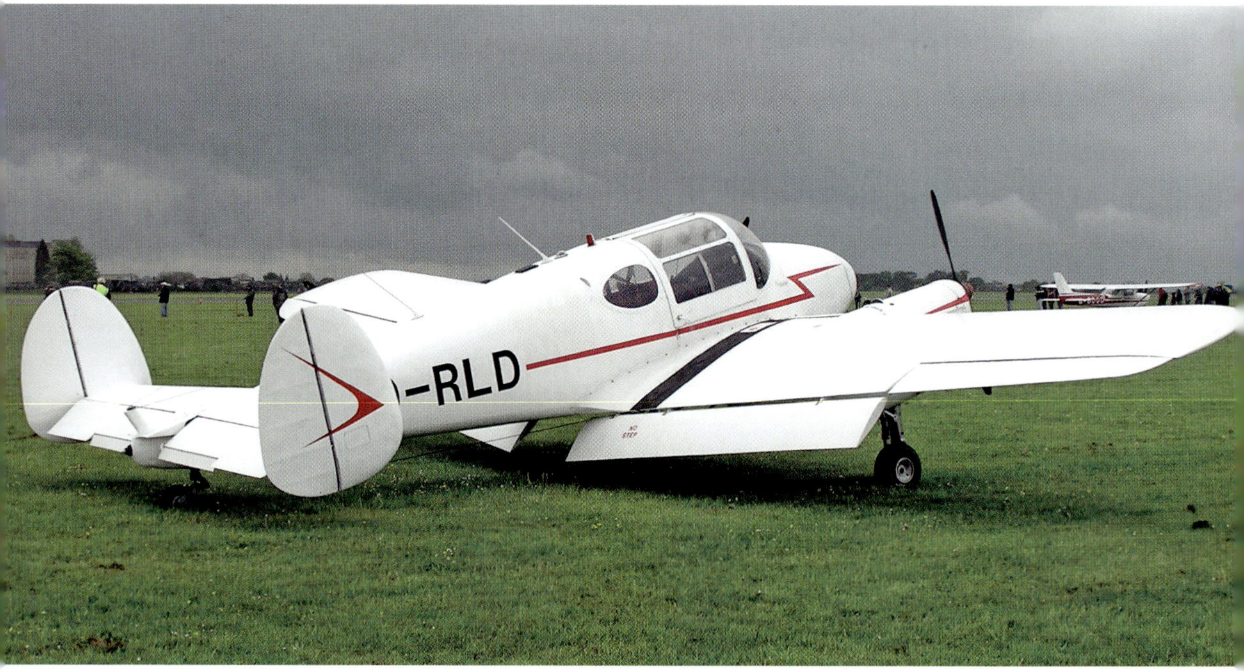

More obvious commercial users included Aer Lingus, Lancashire Aircraft Corporation, BOAC, Starways and several smaller charter companies.

Although Miles Aircraft company had plans for further development of the Gemini, including more powerful engines and redesign of the tail assembly, the company collapsed into bankruptcy in 1947 and its assets, including the Miles Marathon, largely passed to Handley Page.

Percival (Hunting Percival)

In 1916, a young Australian, Edgar Percival, moved to Great Britain to join the Royal Flying Corps. Trained as a pilot, he proved his worth and was promoted to the rank of Captain. He returned to Australia after the Great War but continued his interests in flying, giving joy rides and participating in films.

He came to England again in 1929 and took up the job of test pilot for the Air Ministry. He was also involved in a number of projects with Saunders Roe, but in 1933 he struck out on his own, establishing the Percival Aircraft Company. Its early designs cemented a reputation for record-breaking and racing aircraft, such as the Mew Gull. In 1936, the company was restructured and renamed Percival Aircraft Ltd., and in 1944, the company became part of the Hunting Group and Edgar Percival sold his interests.

In 1936, Percival designed the company's first twin-engine aircraft, the **Percival Q 'Petrel'**. Two versions were envisaged, the Q.4, intended as a four-seat executive aircraft, and the Q.6 six-seat feeder-liner. Only the Q.6 was built; it was a wooden construction with plywood and fabric covering. Powered by two de Havilland Gipsy Six II engines, each of 205hp (153kW), it had a top speed of 195mph (314km/h) and a range of 700 miles (1,130km). Its wingspan was 46ft 8in (14.22m) and the length was 32ft 3in (9.83m).

Despite only a small number being built, the Percival Q 'Petrel' enjoyed international success. (Picryl)

The prototype had its first flight on 14 September 1937 and the first production aircraft was delivered on 2 March 1938; in total, 27 Q6 aircraft were built. Four of the production aircraft were fitted with retractable undercarriages in place of the faired mainwheel structures.

Export strategy was also successful, with Q.6 aircraft going to Iraq, Australia and Egypt. Seven were purchased by the Air Ministry for the RAF, and these were unofficially called the Petrel. Inevitably, at the outbreak of war, most civil aircraft were requestioned for military use. One noteworthy example was the Q.6 operated by Lithuanian Air Lines, which was impressed into Aeroflot after the Soviet Union occupied the Baltic states.

Following the war, surplus Q.6 and Petrel aircraft were sold to civilian users, some being operated by small airlines. In the United Kingdom, Starways and Western Airways were customers.

In the mid-1940s, the company embarked on the design of a twin-engine light airliner to carry five or six passengers, placing considerable emphasis on passenger appeal. The high wing mounting gave excellent visibility for passengers and the tricycle undercarriage meant easy access with a low, level, floor. It was an all-metal stressed skin construction and the undercarriage was retractable.

The aircraft was called the **Percival P.47 Merganser**. It was designed to be powered by de Havilland Gipsy Queen 51 engines, but this proved to be a serious problem because these engines were not available in late 1946 when the fuselage of the prototype was completed. Unfortunately, there were no suitable alternatives available.

However, on 9 May 1947, the Merganser took off for its first flight, powered by Gipsy Queen engines borrowed from the Ministry of Supply. Although the aircraft enabled valuable data to be acquired from flight trials, the Merganser was scrapped in August 1948. A second airframe had been built, but never flew.

The Percival Merganser was obviously not a success, but it did lead to better things. (Alamy)

The Merganser had a wingspan of 47ft 9in (14.55m) and a length of 39ft 8in (12.09m). The borrowed de Havilland Gipsy Queen 51 engines gave it a top speed of 193mph (311km/h) with a range of 800 miles (1,300km).

Although clearly not in itself a success, the lessons learned from the Merganser were embodied in the **Percival P.50 Prince**. This was a larger and heavier aircraft capable of carrying eight passengers. Powered by two Alvis Leonides 501/4 engines, the prototype had its first flight on 13 May 1948.

The Percival Prince was a real success, both in the civilian and military markets. (Alamy)

The prototype was followed by 24 production aircraft in a variety of designations, engines (although all were Alvis Leonides) and modifications to the prototype. The most significant variations were the Prince 2, which had a sloping windscreen and stronger main spar, and the Prince 3, with more powerful engines and lengthened nose on some aircraft.

The Prince was used by operators in many countries including Australia, Brunei and Brazil, as well as European and African countries. The Royal Navy adopted the aircraft as the Sea Prince for training and communications purposes, with 48 being built. The RAF ordered a larger development called the Pembroke for transport functions, and 50 of these were built.

Five civil transport versions of the Pembroke were built as the **Percival P.66 President**. These were powered by two Alvis Leonides 127 radial engines, each delivering 540hp (400kW). The wingspan was 64 6in (19.66m) and the length 46ft (14.02m). The maximum speed was 220mph (350km/h) and the range was 1,03 miles (1,666km).

This aircraft is a Hunting Percival Pembroke, but the civilian version was called the President. (Picryl)

In 1960, Hunting Percival was taken over by British Aircraft Corporation, itself later absorbed into what is now BAE Systems plc.

Chapter 11

Saunders-Roe

amuel Edgar Saunders established a boat-building business based around use of a lightweight material it had developed called Consuta, which was suitable for constructing hulls.

The business moved from Goring on the River Thames to East Cowes on the Isle of Wight and in 1908, the company called S. E. Saunders Ltd was established, with Wolseley Tool and Motor Car Company holding a small interest. The advent of aviation inspired the company to use Consuta as a possible construction material for aircraft, and between 1917 and the late 1920s, Saunders built a number of biplane flying boats as well as a single-engine land biplane.

The company needed additional finance and expertise to continue in the aviation market, and in 1929, Alliott Verdon Roe, together with his business partner, John Lord, and Harold Edgar Broadsmith, invested £42,500 of their own money. They secured investment from other parties and the company was renamed Saunders-Roe Ltd.

In 1928, the new company's first aircraft was the Saunders-Roe A.17 Cutty Sark, an amphibious monoplane; 12 were built and used for predominantly military purposes, although at least two found their way to civil users. More significantly, it paved the way to an enlarged version called the **Saunders-Roe A.19 Cloud**. This was also an amphibious monoplane flying boat with accommodation for a crew of two and eight passengers. Fitted with two Wright J-6 radial engines, each providing 300hp (224kW), the prototype performed its first flight in the middle of 1930. The mounting of the engines on struts above the wing gave ease of access and the capability to install different engines.

The Saunders-Roe A.19 Cloud with the undercarriage wheel visible. (Picryl)

The Air Ministry ordered one aircraft for evaluation as a trainer. Following this, 16 were ordered for training pilots and navigators, designated as the Saunders-Roe A.29. Fitted with Armstrong Siddeley Serval engines, they had room for six students and could carry four 50lb (22.7kg) practice bombs.

The last operational aircraft was retired in July 1939. A total of 22 Clouds had been built, including the military A.29 version. Civilian operators included Czechoslovak State Airlines, Imperial Airways, Guernsey Airways and Jersey Airways.

The A.19 Cloud had a wingspan of 64ft (20m) and a length of 50ft 11½in (15.53m). With the Armstrong Siddeley Serval III engines, the top speed was 118mph (190km/h) and its range was 380 miles (610km).

During its production, a single A.19 Cloud was fitted with three Armstrong Siddeley Lynx IVC engines, together with an additional small aerofoil above the engines and twin fins and rudders. These changes were not successful, and it was re-equipped with two Pratt & Whitney radial engines before delivery. This aircraft was sold to Imperial Airways in 1940 for crew training, but in 1941 it was damaged beyond repair and scrapped. A similar attempt to improve the performance of the Saunders-Roe A.17 Cutty Sark had been made, but failed due to the additional weight on a small airframe.

Undeterred, Saunders-Roe designed a larger aircraft, the **Saunders-Roe A.21 Windhover**, to carry three de Havilland Gipsy II engines, each of 120hp (89kW). Only a prototype and a single production aircraft were built, carrying a crew of two and four to six passengers.

The prototype had its first flight on 16 October 1930. It was delivered to Dominion Airways of New Zealand, but in September 1931 it was sold to Matthews Aviation in Melbourne. From early 1933 to February 1934, it operated between Melbourne and Launceston in Tasmania. This service was via King Island and it was here in May 1936 that it was blown ashore when on charter to a game hunter party. The hull ended its days as an instructional airframe.

The Saunders-Roe A.21 Windhover. This is the prototype aircraft. (Ian McDonell, 1000aircraftphotos.com)

The production aircraft was operated on the Gibraltar to Tangier route by Gibraltar Airways. In May 1935, it was acquired by Jersey Airways, which operated it until its retirement in 1938.

The Windover demonstrates its amphibious capabilities. (Ian Henderson, 1000aircraftphotos.com)

The Windhover had a top speed of 108mph (174km/h) and a range of 400 miles (640km). The wingspan was 54ft 4in (16.56m) and its length was 41ft 4in (12.60m).

Saunders-Roe will long be remembered for innovative designs, including a seaplane jet fighter aircraft and the turboprop-powered Princess flying boat, but after a variety of takeovers, the Saunders-Roe name was lost to aviation.

Chapter 12

Scottish Aviation

Scottish Aviation Ltd was established in Prestwick, Scotland, in 1935. The company originally operated a flying school, but in 1938 it took on maintenance work. During World War Two, this included conversion activity on the Consolidated Liberator bomber.

A milestone was reached in 1950 when the company responded to Air Ministry Specification A.4/45 for a light communication aircraft. The result was the Scottish Aviation Pioneer. After replacing the prototype's disappointing de Havilland Gipsy Queen engine with the more powerful Alvis Leonides, the Pioneer was ordered by the RAF and the air forces of Ceylon (now Sri Lanka), Malaysia and Oman. The Iranian customs authority, meanwhile, operated two Pioneers. A particular attraction was the aircraft's excellent short take-off and landing (STOL) capability, enabling it to take off from unprepared locations in as little as 225ft (69m).

Boosted by the Pioneer's success, Scottish Aviation embarked on the design of a twin-engine version using two Alvis Leonides engines and incorporating the same STOL virtues of its predecessor. A rugged fixed undercarriage helped ensure the aircraft's ability to operate in remote and difficult terrain. The aircraft was aimed at both military and civilian customers. In addition to a crew of two, the Twin Pioneer had accommodation for 16 passengers or up to 12 troops.

The prototype first flew on 25 June 1955. Three pre-production aircraft were constructed for sales demonstrations and trials, after which orders followed, but in 1957, two fatal accidents occurred when outer wing panels detached in flight due to metal fatigue. Redesign solved this problem, but had a negative impact on sales.

Although the Alvis Leonides engine, in several versions, was the predominant choice, six Twin Pioneers were fitted with

The Scottish Aviation Twin Pioneer managed to overcome a number of disasters. (Roger Staker)

Pratt & Whitney R-1340 radial engines, five of which had been ordered by Philippine Air Lines.

Of the 87 Twin Pioneers actually built, the majority were delivered to military users, including the Royal Malaysian Air Force and the Sultan of Oman's Air Force as well as the RAF. Even so, Twin Pioneers served with civilian operators in no less than 20 countries. Some of these operated in remote locations where prepared runways were the exception rather than the rule, the Twin Pioneer's rugged STOL capabilities in this role being highly regarded.

With the 520hp (388kW) Alvis Leonides 514/8 engines, the Twin Pioneer had a top speed of 165mph (266km/h) and a range of 791 miles (1,273km). The wingspan was 76ft 6in (23.32m) and its length was 45ft 3ins (13.70m).

In November 1958, Scottish Aviation Ltd made nearly a third of its employees redundant. In 1977, it merged with Hawker Siddeley and the British Aircraft Corporation to form British Aerospace.

Chapter 13

Short Brothers

The story of Short Brothers began in 1897, when Eustace Short and his brother Oswald started a company to develop and manufacture balloons. The inspiration had occurred when Eustace purchased a second-hand gas-filled balloon. By 1902, they were offering balloons for sale and in 1905, they were successful in securing a contract from the British Indian Army for three observation balloons.

The quality of the brothers' work impressed the superintendent of the Royal Balloon Factory and they were introduced to Charles Rolls (of Rolls-Royce fame), who ordered a large balloon to compete in the 1906 Gordon Bennett Cup Balloon race. More orders followed from members of the Aero Club of Great Britain, and it was through these contacts that Oswald learned of the Wright brothers' flights in Paris in 1908.

Realising that the future lay with powered flight, the third brother, Horace, was persuaded to leave his job and join the partnership, now called Short Brothers. During the Great War, Short Brothers designed and built a successful range of floatplanes that were deployed as far away as the Battle of Gallipoli in 1915. Flying boats were also designed and built, and these would be the forerunners of the company's aircraft in later years. One of these was the military Short Singapore.

Imperial Airways required a flying boat to service its routes between the Mediterranean and India. In response, Short Brothers designed a three-engine flying boat based on the Singapore. It was innovative, being the first British stressed-skin and metal-hulled flying boat, where the aircraft skin takes part of the structural load. Power was provided by three Bristol Jupiter IXF radial engines, each delivering 540hp (400kW).

There was a crew of three, two pilots sitting in an open cockpit together with a radio operator who was fortunate enough to share the passenger compartment with up to 15 passengers. The **Short S.8 Calcutta** made its first flight on 14 February 1928. It had actually been launched the day before, but left overnight to check for leakage!

In March, the Calcutta was delivered to the Marine Aircraft Experimental Establishment for trials to assess both the airworthiness and sea-handling capabilities of the aircraft. These were completed by 27 July and the Calcutta was flown back to Short Brothers. On 1 August, it flew to Westminster, landing on the River Thames between Vauxhall Bridge and Lambeth Bridge. Here it was inspected by Members of Parliament, including Winston Churchill, who was then Chancellor of the Exchequer. Members of the House of Lords also toured the Calcutta.

The Short S.8 Calcutta helped establish air routes from Britain to India. (Picryl)

It was formally handed over to Imperial Airways on 9 August and the airline inaugurated its Mediterranean to Karachi leg of its Britain to India route with the Calcutta later in 1928.

A total of seven Short S.8 Calcutta flying boats were built. The French aircraft manufacturer Breguet purchased one in 1924 and developed a military version for the French Navy. It was similar to Short's own military development, which became the Short Rangoon.

Flying was not without incident. On 26 October 1929, a Calcutta on a scheduled flight from Naples to Genoa made a forced landing off La Spezia, Italy. Unfortunately, the weather was poor that day, with high winds. During the attempt to tow the flying boat ashore, it sank, killing all seven people on board.

A little after nightfall on 31 December 1935, a Calcutta was approaching the end of its flight from Crete to Alexandria, Egypt, when all three engines stopped. Nine passengers and three crew members were killed by impact with the water or by drowning, the pilot being the only survivor. An Air Ministry inquiry concluded that the carburettors had been adjusted in a way that had increased fuel consumption, causing the engines to fail due to loss of fuel.

The Calcutta had a top speed of 118mph (190km/h) and a range of 650 miles (1,050km). Its wingspan was 93ft (28.35m) and its length 66ft 9in (20.35m).

In the early 1930s, Short Brothers designed and developed a light transport aircraft that proved ideal for use on small airstrips, of which there were many. The straightforward design was of a high-wing monoplane with accommodation for a pilot and up to six passengers. The fuselage and wings were metal with fabric covering and the twin powerplants were small air-cooled radial engines provided by Pobjoy Airmotors and Aircraft Ltd.

The prototype **Short S.16 Scion** made its first flight on 18 August 1933. There was sufficient interest from potential operators to warrant the commencement of production. The prototype had been fitted with Pobjoy R engines of 80hp (60kW) but the production aircraft had Pobjoy Niagara III motors of 90hp (67kW). The Scion was made available as either a landplane or a floatplane, so allowing operation from lakes and watercourses.

An Australia-based Short S.16 Scion keeps a Monospar company. (Picryl)

After the first five aircraft, including the prototype, improvements were made and the remaining 17 aircraft were designated the Short Scion II. The most significant change was the repositioning of the engines so that the thrust line was in alignment with the chord-line of the wings. This eliminated much changing of trim when power was increased or decreased. Improvements were also made to the cabin windows and the windscreen.

The fifth production Scion II was kept by Short Brothers for experimental purposes. At one stage, it was fitted with slender wooden wings as part of the company's planning for a future aircraft. These wings had flaps that increased the chord and wing area when activated. They were called Gouge flaps after the Short Brothers engineer Arthur Gouge, who invented them. Tests showed that they did indeed decrease the take-off distance and the stalling speed.

A Short Scion of West of Scotland Airways. (Bernard Harding Collection)

The last six Scion II aircraft were built by Pobjoy under licence and in 1935, that company was acquired by Short Brothers. The very last Scion was built in late 1937. Operators were located in Australia, Aden, Sierra Leone, Palestine and the UK. As expected, these were small independent airlines often operating in remote regions. Papuan Concessions Ltd and Elders Colonial Airways Ltd of Sierra Leone both operated floatplanes. The British-based aircraft were impressed into the RAF during World War Two.

With the Pobjoy Niagara engines, the top speed of the Scion was 128mph (206km/h). Its wingspan was 42ft (12.80m) and the length was 31ft 6in (9.60m).

In late 1932, Imperial Airways wished to add to its fleet of Handley Page HP.42 aircraft. However, Handley Page quoted a price that Imperial Airways would not accept. Instead, the airline approached Short Brothers for an alternative large (by contemporary terms) airliner.

The solution offered was a land-based development of an existing Short flying boat, the Short Kent. By using the wings and other flying surfaces of the Kent, married to a new fuselage, an airliner capable of carrying a crew of four and 39 passengers was produced. This was the **Short L.17 Scylla**.

The aircraft had an all-metal framework and the four engines were carried between the lower and upper wings, mounted on struts. The engine nacelles were thoughtfully designed to accept a variety of Bristol engines without the need for modification.

Imperial Airways ordered two Scyllas in 1933 for use on its London to Paris and other European city routes. The first flight took place on 26 March 1934, with the aircraft being powered by Bristol Jupiter XFBM radial engines of 555hp (414kW). When one of the aircraft was severely damaged by crosswinds at Brussels airport, it was re-fitted with Bristol Pegasus XC engines giving 660hp (490kW).

The Short L.17 Scylla. This one is actually named *Scylla*. (Ed Coates, 1000aircraftphotos.com)

Both of the Short Scylla aircraft continued in use by Imperial Airways until the airline was merged with BOAC in 1939. They were taken out of service in 1940, one having been wrecked and the other scrapped.

With the Bristol Jupiter engines, the top speed was 137mph (220km/h). The Scylla had a wingspan of 113ft (34.44m) and a length of 83ft 10in (25.55m).

Global air passenger and freight transport was expanding rapidly in the early 1930s. Imperial Airways was more than keen to secure its market share and needed an aircraft capable of meeting the burgeoning demand. The airline's technical adviser, Major Robert Hobart Mayo, envisaged an aircraft with the ability to carry both passengers and cargo throughout the world, and, more specifically, a passenger capacity of 24 in considerable comfort and with space for airmail and freight. It should have a cruising speed of 170mph (270km/h) and a range of at least 700 miles (1,100km). It was also expected to allow for an extended range to serve a North Atlantic route. This meant it needed to be able to cover 2,000 miles (3,200km).

Short Brothers was well known to Imperial Airways and was doubtless seen as a likely provider of what was clearly an innovative but risky venture. There was initial reluctance on the part of Short Brothers, because the haste with which the airline wished to have aircraft in service did not permit the usual procedures of prototyping and testing. However, Imperial Airways was insistent that delay was unacceptable and in 1935, the airline placed an order for 28 flying boats of a type yet to be designed.

The design team was led by Arthur Gouge. It soon became apparent that the necessary scale and weight of the potential aircraft would determine some of the features; the necessary propeller clearance from water would mean a high wing mounting, while the anticipated 18-tonne (just under 20 tons) weight ruled out Short Brothers' conventional wide-bottomed hulls, which would create excessive drag.

The basic layout that emerged was similar to the Short Scion floatplane. The experimental wing that had been flown on Short Brothers' own Scion served as a template for the new design. Even so, what was being attempted was unique in the British aircraft industry as no aircraft of the scale and complexity had hitherto been constructed. For example, Short Brothers had to develop machinery to produce the main wing spars.

In 1936, the Air Ministry established a new company based in Belfast. It was called Short & Harland Ltd and was owned by Harland and Wolff and Short Brothers as equal 50 per cent shareholders.

The aircraft that appeared was the **Short Empire**, a four-engine monoplane flying boat with a wingspan of 114ft (34.75m) and a length of 88ft (26.82m). It had its first flight on 3 July 1936 and was delivered to Imperial Airways, with a proving flight to Marseille, on 22 October. This aircraft undertook its first operational revenue-earning flight on 6 February 1937.

This first version, the Short S.23 Empire, could carry a crew of five and up to 17 passengers, together with 4,480lb (2,035kg) of cargo. It was powered by four Bristol Pegasus X radial engines, each of 920hp (690kW). These gave a maximum speed of 200mph (320km/h) and a range of 760 miles (1,220km).

The second Empire was the first example of the long-range version. It had its maiden flight on 15 September 1936 and was delivered to Imperial Airways on 4 December. There followed a series of maiden flights and deliveries at the rate of one a month, but the last three Empire flying boats ordered by Imperial Airways were diverted in September 1938 to Qantas Empire Airways.

Above: The Short Empire pioneered long-distance air travel in considerable luxury for its day. (Picryl)

Left: The cabin in the Short Empire. (Picryl)

During early 1937, Imperial Airways was able to operate the Empire flying boats on some very long-distance routes. These included from Calshot in Hampshire to Alexandria, Egypt, a distance of 2,300 miles (3,700km). In mid-July, the first transatlantic flight of an Empire took place, from Foynes in Ireland to Botwood in Newfoundland, a distance of 1,993 miles (3,207km) and a clear demonstration of the potential for long-distance, non-stop air travel.

Such was Imperial Airways' satisfaction with the Short Empire that towards the end of 1937, the company placed an order for an additional 11 aircraft. At that time, the total order of 39 aircraft was the single largest order to have been placed for a British civil aircraft. Eight of the new order aircraft were designated as the S.30 Empire. These carried four Bristol Perseus XIIc sleeve-valve engines which, although of lower horsepower (890hp, 660kW), were more efficient and had a smaller-diameter nacelle that reduced drag.

The S.30 also benefited from a stronger airframe and a heavier gauge of sheeting for the fuselage and wings, allowing an increase in take-off weight. This increased the range to 1,500 miles (2,400km). The last three S.30 aircraft were transferred to Tasman Empire Airways Ltd, and the very last of 42 Short Empire flying boats was delivered to Imperial Airways in March 1940.

Four of the S.30 Empires were fitted with in-flight refuelling equipment, together with extra fuel tanks so that they could be used on transatlantic flights. The drawback was a reduction in payload from 6,250 (2,830kg) to 4,270lb (1,940kg). The refuelling 'tankers' were three modified Handley Page Harrow bombers. One of these operated from Ireland and another from Newfoundland, off the coast of Canada.

In 1939, Imperial Airways placed another order for three modified S.30 Empires designated as S.33. Although the same construction as the S.30, this new series had the latest Bristol Pegasus XI engines. Only two were completed and delivered to Imperial Airways' successor, BOAC.

It is perhaps what was inside the Empire flying boat that is as interesting as its modern, clean appearance and efficiency. The hull was 17ft (5.2m) deep and contained two decks. The upper deck was for freight and mail, together with storage space and an office for the ship's clerk, in which were the controls for ventilation, fuse boxes, circuit switches and fuel cocks. At the front of the lower deck was the marine storage area for an anchor, drogues, boat hook and a mooring bollard. Behind this was the forward passenger cabin, followed by a corridor with toilets and galley. This was followed in turn by the aft cabin. The cabins could accommodate comfortable seats or bunks for sleeping. Finally, another compartment for freight or mail extended into the rear of the fuselage.

The Short S.33 Empire used by BOAC. (Picryl)

The flying crew of two pilots and the navigator shared a spacious flight deck, which was called 'the bridge'. Instrumentation was very good for its time and an autopilot was installed. The fifth member of the crew was the steward.

Between 1937 and 1943, a number of Empires were lost to accidents or enemy action. Landing or take-off crashes accounted for three incidents, in which a total of ten lives were lost. Carburettor icing caused one aircraft to ditch in the Atlantic Ocean, where it sank with the loss of three lives. In January 1942, a BOAC Empire operated by Qantas was shot down by seven Japanese fighters, killing 13 of the 18 on board. Finally, in April 1943, a Qantas-operated aircraft was shot down by Japanese naval fighters and all on board were killed.

When World War Two began, two Empire flying boats were modified with gun turrets and air-to-surface vessel radar and used by RAF Coastal Command. The Empire's more important military contribution was seen in the Short Sunderland, a close relative of the civil airliner. By 1948, all the Short Empires had been destroyed or scrapped.

Imperial Airways' primary objective for the Empire was to service the routes to South Africa and Australia. However, there was pressure from the USA to provide a transatlantic service. Although in-flight refuelling could achieve this, it came at the price of carrying fewer passengers and less cargo.

To solve this problem, Imperial Airways' Major Robert Mayo made a proposal that many at the time would have found eccentric at best. This was to mount a relatively small long-range seaplane on top of a large 'mother' aircraft, which would take off and release the smaller aircraft to continue the flight. In fairness to Major Mayo, this concept had been tried in May 1916, when a Felixstowe Porte Baby carried a Bristol Scout Fighter aloft to 1,000ft (305m) where it was detached and flew back safely.

The Air Ministry gave its blessing with Specification 13/33, and so began the Short Mayo composite project. Two new aircraft were designed and developed, the first being a variant of the trusted Empire flying boat, but with greatly modified hull and wings. Specifically, the wings had a greater area to provide the lift required, and the engines were situated further from the hull. The rear fuselage was swept up to raise the tailplane. This aircraft was designated the Short S.21 Maia. It could carry 18 passengers and first flew on 27 July 1937. The combination of the two aircraft, a 'mother ship' and a 'daughter' was called Mayo, after its inventor.

The Short Mayo piggyback combination. The mother aircraft is the Short S.21 Maia. (Johan Visschedijk, 1000aircraftphotos.com)

A structure was built on top of the hull to carry the smaller floatplane, the **Short S.20 Mercury**. This was a twin-float, four-engine aircraft with a crew of two, the pilot and a navigator, who sat in tandem position. It was capable of carrying 1,000lb (450kg) of airmail. The fuel tanks held 1,200 gallons (5,500 litres, 1,400 US gallons) of fuel.

In order to minimise risk, the flight controls were locked in neutral positions until separation. The only exception was for the elevator and rudder trim tabs. Mercury's maiden flight was on 5 September 1937.

The Short S.20 Mercury. (Johan Visschedijk, 1000aircraftphotos.com)

When in position on top of Maia, both pilots (Maia and Mercury) had control over locks that held the two aircraft in place. Even so, there was inevitably slight movement; a system of lights indicated when Mercury was in balance fore and aft so that trim changes could be made accordingly. When they were satisfied, both pilots released their respective locks, but an automatic third lock would only operate when sufficient acceleration had been achieved, the measurement being 3,000lbf (13,000 Newtons). At this point, Maia would drop and Mercury would climb to give maximum separation. Similar rules apply to glider release from a towing aircraft.

On 6 February 1938, the first successful release of Mercury from Maia in flight took place. There were further successful test flights and on 21 July 1938, the first transatlantic flight was made, taking off from Foynes in Ireland and landing at Boucherville, near Montreal. Maia was carrying ten passengers and luggage. The complete journey took 20 hours 21 minutes, meaning an average speed over the ground of 144mph (232km/h).

Imperial Airways continued the Maia/Mercury combination, with flights to Alexandria in Egypt and a record flight of 6,045 miles (9,729km) from Dundee in Scotland to Alexander Bay in South Africa in October 1938, albeit with some modification to Mercury to extend its range.

Mercury had a wingspan of 73ft (22.25m) and a length of 51ft (15.54m). Powered by four Napier Rapier VI engines, each of 365hp (272kW), it had a maximum speed of 212mph (341km/h). Its normal range was 3,900 miles (6,300km).

Maia carried a crew of three. Its wingspan was 114ft (34.75m) and its length 84ft 11ins (25.88m). Power was delivered by four Bristol Pegasus XC engines of 919hp (685kW) each, giving a top speed of 200mph (320km/h) and a range of 850 miles (1,370km).

Maia was destroyed by German bombers in Poole harbour on 11 May 1941, while Mercury was transferred to the RAF, but was broken up in August 1941 so that the aluminium could be re-used.

The Empire flying boat had been considered a very successful aircraft that had proved wrong those who had believed that a flying boat of its size would not be capable of flight. Apparently, some of these sceptics were employed by the Marine Aircraft Experimental Establishment, an organisation with an important role in marine aircraft development. Even so, there was recognition that such an aircraft would have both civil and military advantages. A particular concept that found favour was the idea of having a large flying boat with a strengthened hull sufficient to permit catapult-assisted take-offs. This would support long-distance flights for mail and patrol purposes.

Late in the 1930s, Imperial Airways asked Short & Harland to consider designing a larger version of the Empire, one that could carry both passengers and airmail between Ireland and Newfoundland without having to stop for fuel. Coincidentally, the Air Ministry had issued Specification 14/38, looking for a long-range transport or airliner with a pressurised cabin for high-altitude flight and Short Brothers had been invited to provide a tender. Both potential opportunities were of interest to the company.

Work on what would become the **Short S.26** began in earnest and Imperial Airways placed an order for three aircraft. At about the same time, the Air Ministry lost its interest in catapults, but provided a subsidy to Imperial Airways for its purchase of the S.26.

The design of this new aircraft was effectively an enlarged version of the Empire, but it benefited from features that were being built into the military Short Sunderland. Weight reduction was a key theme of the design and construction as it was expected to cross the Atlantic without refuelling and therefore was intended to form the backbone of Imperial Airways' transatlantic services.

The aircraft were delivered with no interior finish as they were intended for carrying just airmail. However, the airline had plans to use the three aircraft in different ways, the first as a long-haul mail service, the second as a medium-haul aircraft with perhaps a dozen passengers, and the third as a relatively short-haul aircraft with 24 passengers.

The Short S.26 was quickly commandeered by the RAF. (Philip Lund, 1000aircraftphotos.com)

The S.26 was powered by four Bristol Hercules radial engines, each of 1,400hp (1,000kW). The fuel tanks located in the wings could carry 3,600 gallons (16,000 litres, 4,300 US gallons). A crew of five was seated in a larger cockpit than in the Empire.

The Short S.26 made its first flight on 21 July 1939 and it was delivered to Imperial Airways on 24 September. This was not a good time to be launching a new, large, civil aircraft into operational service, however; within a few days of its delivery, Imperial Airways was told that all three S.26 aircraft would be impressed into RAF service, along with their crews. In February 1940, the second aircraft was completed, and in July 1940 the third and final S.26 followed suit.

All three aircraft were modified to military standards and from 1941 they served with the RAF, predominantly flying supplies to Gibraltar and the Middle East to keep other aircraft maintained. The second S.26 was lost on 20 June 1941, following a heavy landing off Cape Finisterre when two engines failed. In December 1941, the remaining pair were returned to what was now BOAC and fitted with 40 seats of basic configuration so as to provide transport between Great Britain and Nigeria.

The third S.26 was lost over Lisbon in January 1943, following an engine seizure and fire. The last surviving aircraft was used by BOAC on routes to West Africa until its retirement in 1947. It ended its days moored at Rochester Harbour until, in 1954, it ran aground when on tow and was scrapped.

The development of the Short Empire flying boat was closely followed by one of the most famous flying boats of World War Two, the Sunderland. During its production from 1938 to 1946, no less than 749 Sunderlands were built and these saw service with the RAF and many other air forces, together with the French Navy.

As could be expected, when the demand for civil aerial transport grew, the potential for commercial use of the Sunderland began to be realised. In late 1942, BOAC had already acquired six Sunderland Mk III flying boats that had been built as non-military aircraft on the production line. They could carry 22 passengers and two tons (1,814kg) of cargo or 16 passengers and 3 tons (2,722kg) of freight. They were used on routes to Nigeria and India. A further six were acquired in 1943.

Late in the war, BOAC purchased further Sunderlands, but modified them to provide better passenger accommodation and refinement. These aircraft were designated as the **Short Hythe** and BOAC operated 29 converted aircraft by the end of the war. The Mk III was selected as the basis for the Hythe because the configuration of its revised hull improved seaworthiness. The Hythe was powered by four Bristol Pegasus XVIII radial engines, each producing 1,065hp (794kW). The wingspan was 112ft 9½in (34.38m) and the length 85ft 4ins (26.01m). The Hythe had a top speed of 210mph (340km/h) and a range of 1,780 miles (2,860km).

The Short Hythe was another post-war solution to a rapidly emerging need. (Alamy)

It was obvious to Short & Harland and to operators of the Hythe that it was a stop-gap, being effectively a very basic conversion of a military aircraft rather than a purpose-built commercial machine. An example was the fairing over of the gun turrets, which did little for the aerodynamics and appearance. Even so, the Sunderland was a proven base on which to develop and, when the war ended, examples were in plentiful supply.

In November 1945, Short & Harland flew a more thoughtfully converted Sunderland with a refurbished interior and new, low-drag fairings over the nose and tail. This aircraft entered service with BOAC in June 1946, having received a certificate of airworthiness. BOAC was keen to have all its Sunderland-based flying boats brought up to airliner standards and issued an order for the 'new' version, which was now called the **Short Sandringham**.

While the first had been based on the Mk III Sunderland with its Bristol Pegasus engines, what was now delivered was based on the Sunderland Mk V, with four Pratt & Whitney Twin Wasp engines that produced 1,200hp (890kW) each. These gave the Sandringham a top speed of 206 (332km/h) and a range of 2,440 miles (3,930km).

The Sandringham carried a crew of five and up to 22 passengers. It could carry 16 'sleeping' passengers. The wingspan was the same as the Hythe, but the new fairings front and back increased the length to 86ft 3in (26.29m).

The Short Sandringham was another conversion of the trusty Sunderland. (Alamy)

About 20 Sandringham conversions were made, going on to serve with Aerolineas Argentinas, Ansett and Qantas in Australia, Tasman Empire Airways, Norwegian Airlines, Compania Aeronautica Uruguaya, BOAC and Antilles Air Boats based in the US Virgin Islands. This last operator flew the Sandringham into the 1970s.

The final member of the Empire/Sunderland lineage was developed in 1946 from the Short Seaford long-range maritime bomber, which itself was a development of the Sunderland. Although some were conversions of Seafords, there were 16 new-build examples of this new flying boat, which was called the **Short S.45A Solent**. It first flew on 11 November 1946.

Powered by four Bristol Hercules 637 engines of 1,690hp (1,260kW) each, it had a top speed of 273mph (439km/h) and a range of 1,800 miles (2,900km). The Solent had accommodation for a crew of seven and 24 day and night passengers or 36 day passengers. There were four cabins on the lower deck and two on the upper deck. The upper deck also had a lounge and dining area adjacent to a kitchen. The lower deck had toilets, dressing rooms and three cargo compartments.

The ultimate offspring of the Empire was the Short S.45A Solent. (Picryl)

In 1948, BOAC introduced the Solent II on its services between Southampton and Johannesburg. These were effectively civilian conversions of the Short Seaford, providing for a crew of seven and 34 passengers. There were three flights each week and the journey took four days with, of course, overnight stops. The service had been operated by Avro Yorks, so the route was well established. The service with the Solent ended on 10 November 1950.

Tasman Empire Airways Ltd operated one Solent II and four Solent IV flying boats. The Solent IVs were powered by Bristol Hercules 733 engines providing 2,040hp (1,521kW) and had a range of 3,000 miles (4,830km). They were configured to provide accommodation for 44 passengers. Between 1949 and 1960, they provided scheduled services between Sydney, Fiji, Auckland and Wellington. The final Solent service was on 14 September 1960.

In addition to BOAC, an independent British airline, Aquila Airways, operated the Solent using ex-BOAC and Tasman aircraft. The services were between Southampton and Madeira and the Canary Islands. A fatal accident occurred on 15 November 1957, when an Aquila Airways Solent crashed near Chessell, a village on the Isle of Wight. Of the 58 people on board, 45 were killed. When Aquila withdrew its Madeira service on 30 September 1958, it marked the end of British commercial flying boat operations.

The Short Solent II had a wingspan of 112ft 9ins (34.37m) and a length of 87ft 8in (26.72m).

In 1977, the company changed its name back to Short Brothers and became a public limited company in 1984. It was sold by the British government to Bombardier in June 1989.

Chapter 14

Spartan

British aviation pioneer Sir Oliver Simmonds designed and constructed a prototype aircraft in 1928., calling it the Simmonds Spartan. It was a successful design and it is believed that more than 50 were built. However, there arose financial difficulties that required external investment, resulting in the establishment of a company called Spartan Aircraft Ltd in 1930.

In 1931, the investor Whitehall Securities Corporation Ltd acquired a significant holding in Saunders-Roe Ltd. In practice, this resulted in a virtual merger of Spartan into Saunders-Roe. This was a time of emerging names in the field of aviation and in the case of Saunders-Roe, an important associate and business partner was an Australian aircraft designer named Edgar Percival. One of his creations was the three-engine Saro-Percival Mailplane, a monoplane with wooden wings and plywood-covered fuselage. Power came from three de Havilland Gipsy III engines of 120hp (89kW) each.

After Percival sold his interest in the aircraft to Saunders-Roe and established his own aircraft company, Saunders-Roe transferred development to Spartan and renamed the aircraft the Spartan Mailplane. It was modified to include two passenger seats. In June 1932, it was flown from Blackpool to Karachi (then in India) taking 5 days, 23 hours and 50 minutes. It would doubtless have been seen as a great achievement. Even so, there was still no commercial interest expressed in the Mailplane.

However, the basic design had been developed to produce a passenger transport for six passengers and a crew of two. The original layout of a low-wing monoplane had been retained, but the fuselage was now an all-metal structure. The new design was designated the **Spartan Cruiser** and it had its maiden flight in May 1932.

In June 1932, the Cruiser and the Mailplane were demonstrated at the Society of British Aircraft Constructors show at Hendon. There followed an extensive European demonstration tour covering nearly 3,600 miles (5,800km), resulting in an order for two aircraft from Aeroput, a Yugoslavian airline. There was also a licence opportunity with Yugoslavia-based Fabrika aeroplana i hidroaviona Zmaj to build further examples.

An extensive redesign took place; the resulting definitive aircraft, with a modified cockpit and fuselage, was known as the Spartan Cruiser II and the first example was flown in February 1933, powered by three Cirrus Hermes IV engines. This engine choice was also followed for two other Cruisers. Two more were fitted with a Czechoslovak-designed Walter Major engine, but the majority of the 17 Spartan Cruisers built were fitted with the Gipsy Major engines. In the event, only one aircraft was built by the licensee.

A Spartan Cruiser, in its day a comfortable small airliner. (Picryl)

The interior of the Cruiser was well planned for its time, with comfortable seating arranged along the sides of the cabin. In addition to the windows, illumination was provided by roof lights. The side windows could slide open for ventilation and there were celluloid roof windows. Behind the passenger cabin was a space for luggage.

Spartan Air Lines Ltd was established to operate three Cruisers between London (Heston) and Cowes on the Isle of Wight. These operated between 1933 and 1935. Other British operators included British Airways Ltd, Northern and Scottish Airways, Railway Air Services and United Airways. In 1940, three Cruisers were impressed into the RAF.

The Spartan Cruiser II with de Havilland Gipsy Major engines had a wingspan of 54ft (16.46m) and a length of 39ft 2in (11.94m). The top speed was 133mph (214km/h) and it had a range of 310 miles (499km).

The Cruiser was the last aircraft to carry the Spartan name.

Chapter 15

Supermarine

In 1913, Noel Pemberton-Billing set up a business near Southampton to build motor launches. Later, the company began to design and build aircraft. Upon his election as a Member of Parliament in 1916, he decided to sell the company to his factory manager, Hubert Scott-Paine, who renamed it Supermarine Aviation Works Ltd.

In 1917, the company appointed a young engineer called Reginald Joseph Mitchell, and in 1920 he became the chief engineer.

As the company name implies, Supermarine was largely focused on seaplanes and in early 1923, Mitchell designed an amphibious flying boat to carry passengers. The primary requirement was to meet the needs of the British Marine Air Navigation Company Ltd, an airline that was a joint venture between Supermarine and Southern Railway. The airline wanted the aircraft for routes from Southampton to the Channel Islands and to France.

Three aircraft, called the **Supermarine Sea Eagle**, were built, with the first flight taking place in June 1923. Although no routes to France actually materialised, the first service to Guernsey commenced on 25th September 1923. This was Britain's first scheduled flying boat service.

The Supermarine Sea Eagle, designed by an aviation legend. (Alamy)

The first aircraft was destroyed in a crash on 21 May 1924. Another was rammed by a ship in the harbour at St Peter Port, Guernsey, and destroyed. The remaining Sea Eagle continued to serve the route until 1928, when it was replaced. By then, it was being operated by Imperial Airways, following that company's creation in 1924 by the merger of airlines.

The Sea Eagle was powered by a Rolls-Royce Eagle IX water-cooled engine generating 360hp (270kW). This gave the aircraft a top speed of 93mph (150km/h) and a range of 230 miles (370km). The wingspan was 46ft (14m) and the Sea Eagle's length was 37ft 4in (11.38m). It had a crew of two (the pilot and a mechanic) and capacity for up to six passengers. The inclusion of a mechanic in the crew is interesting!

In 1928, Supermarine was acquired by Vickers Ltd and renamed Supermarine Aviation Works (Vickers) Ltd. The Supermarine name and the genius of R. J. Mitchell would survive to create arguably the most famous and iconic British aircraft of all time, the Spitfire. Sadly, Mitchell did not live long enough to see his creation go into production.

An Imperial Airways Supermarine Sea Eagle takes to the sky. (Alamy)

Chapter 16

Vickers

Vickers was established as an engineering company in 1828 and became a public company in 1867 as Vickers, Sons and Company. During the latter part of the 19th century, diversification took place and then, in 1911, the name changed to Vickers Ltd and its business operations expanded to include aircraft manufacture.

During the Great War, Vickers designed and built single-engine military biplanes with both pusher and tractor engines. As the nature of the war changed and the technology available to both sides improved, the options for the type of aircraft needed and that were appropriate also changed. In July 1917, the Air Board, which was responsible for managing the Royal Flying Corps and, later, the Royal Air Force, responded to German air raids on London by ordering heavy bombers from Handley Page. It also ordered prototype heavy bombers from Handley Page and Vickers.

This was followed in August 1917 by an order for three prototypes from Vickers. Such was the pace of development that the first of these had its maiden flight in November 1917. However, there were challenges to be faced with regard to the engines and indeed, the second prototype crashed due to engine failure. It was not until October 1918 that the fourth prototype, fitted with Rolls-Royce Eagle engines, became the standard for production of the Vickers Vimy. Although too late to have an impact on the war, the Vimy became the RAF's standard bomber until 1925.

The Vimy had proven itself on long-distance flights, including the first transatlantic aerial crossing in June 1919 by John Alcock and Arthur Brown. Given the anticipated demand for civilian air transport post-war, both passenger and cargo, an aircraft based on the Vimy's proven airframe and engines was a sensible development.

The resulting aircraft was the **Vickers Vimy Commercial**. It had a fuselage of larger diameter than its bomber counterpart, allowing for a cabin that could accommodate 10 passengers. Construction was largely of spruce plywood, and the Rolls-Royce Eagle VIII engines, each of 300hp (220kW), were retained.

The prototype had its first flight on 13 April 1919. It was entered into the 1920 Britain to Cape Town air race and left its home base of Brooklands, Surrey, on 24 January. It reached Tanganyika, now Tanzania, but crashed on take-off at Tabora. All five occupants survived. The accident was due to failure of the starboard engine at low altitude.

A large order for Vickers aircraft was placed in 1919 by the Chinese government. The order included 100 Vimy Commercials, but this was reduced to 40 when the contract was actually signed in 1920. Although 43 is the number of Vimy Commercials thought to have been delivered to China, it is believed that only seven saw civilian use, and it is suggested that the other aircraft remained in crates.

The Vimy Commercial, as its name implies, was a civilian variant of the Great War Vickers Vimy bomber. (Picryl)

Other civilian operators included Grands Express Amiens (a French airline), Instone Air Line and Imperial Airways. Each of these flew only one Vimy Commercial. With the Rolls-Royce Eagle VIII engines, the top speed was 100mph (160km/h) with a range of 900 miles (1,400km). Although dimensions specifically for the Vimy Commercial are not available, the Vimy Mk II on which it was based had a wingspan of 68in (20.75m) and a length of 43ft 7in (13.28m).

Concurrent with work on the Vickers Vimy Commercial, Vickers began research into amphibious aircraft. In December 1918, the company used an experimental tank at St Albans in Hertfordshire to test various fuselage designs. A prototype five-seat-cabin biplane was built, powered by a single 275hp (205kW) Rolls-Royce Falcon III engine mounted in pusher format under the upper wing. It first flew in 1919.

On 18 December 1919, a tragedy occurred. Sir John Alcock was flying the prototype, now called the **Vickers Type 54 Viking**, to the Paris exhibition. It was foggy when he put in to land at Côte d'Evrard, close to Rouen in Normandy, and the Viking crashed, claiming the life of one of the world's true aviation pioneers. Nevertheless, the Viking's potential for both military and civil use was recognised. A further two aircraft were constructed, incorporating modifications including a greater wingspan and different engines. These were given the titles Viking II and Viking III. Then came the Type 54 Viking IV, which was the production aircraft. Of the 31 Vikings constructed, this version accounted for 26. Military and civilian users operated the type in Argentina, Canada, France, Japan, Netherlands, the USSR and the United States as well as Great Britain. Two operated as civilian aircraft in Great Britain, but one of these was lost in a fatal accident on 13 April 1922.

The Vickers Type 54 Viking was widely used by operators across the world. (Alamy)

The Viking IV with a 450hp (336kW) Napier Lion engine had a top speed of 113mph (182km/h) and a range of 925 miles (1,480km). Its wingspan was 50ft (15.24m) and its length was 34ft 2in (10.41m). It could carry a pilot and four passengers.

The designer of the Vickers Vimy, Reginald (Rex) Pierson, designed what was a more truly civilian aircraft based on the Vimy bomber. It was a biplane airliner flown by a single pilot who sat in an open cockpit, and incorporated a cabin with seating for six to eight passengers. Unlike the Vimy, this aircraft, or, more accurately, the first six of the eight built, was powered by a single Rolls-Royce Eagle VIII engine. These were low-cost war-surplus engines producing 360hp (268kW). The remaining two aircraft had 450hp (336kW) Napier Lion engines installed, which improved performance.

The fuselage was a very tall oval-shaped construction and filled the space between the upper and lower wings. This aircraft was called the **Vickers Vulcan**, but its unusual shape earned it the somewhat impolite name of the 'Flying Pig'.

The 'Flying Pig' nickname was probably justifiable for the Vickers Vulcan. (Picryl)

The Vulcan's first flight was in April 1922 and in August of that year, the first example was delivered to Instone Airlines. This airline was absorbed into Imperial Airways and that company operated the Vulcan on its European service. A single Vulcan was supplied to Qantas, but was returned by the airline because of its poor performance. There were also reliability problems, and only one or two Vulcans stayed in service beyond the mid-1920s.

The very last Vulcan, owned by Imperial Airways, crashed during a flight to test a new engine on 13 July 1928. It was carrying a pilot and five passengers, made up of members of staff and a government aeronautical inspector. The engine overheated and lost power, with the result that the Vulcan crashed into a potato field and the engine caught fire. The pilot and one passenger survived, but four were killed.

The Vulcan had a wingspan of 49ft (14.94m) and a length of 38ft (11.58m). It stood at a height of 14ft 3in (4.34m) above the ground. With the Napier Lion engine, the Vulcan's top speed was 112mph (180km/h) and had a range of 460 miles (740km).

Post-war military aircraft development by Vickers had seen the production of large twin-engine bomber and transport aircraft, one of the latter being the Vickers Type 56 Victoria, which had its first flight in 1922. Instone Airlines expressed interest in a commercial airliner based on the Victoria, while the Air Ministry issued Specification 1/22 and invited Vickers to tender for a 23-seat passenger aircraft.

The resulting **Vickers Vanguard** had a wider fuselage than the Victoria and was originally powered by two Napier Lion engines. During the manufacturer's tests, these were replaced by Rolls-Royce Condor III engines, each of 650hp (485kW). During its first flight on 18 July 1923, the aircraft was found to be tail-heavy. This was resolved by altering the tail plane angle.

As testing and changes took place, the Vanguard received new 'Type' numbers, with the final configuration being designated the Vickers Type 96 Vanguard. In 1925, it was described as the World's largest passenger aeroplane. Final trials at the Aeroplane and Armament Experimental Establishment were concluded to much praise and in May 1928, the Vanguard was handed over to Imperial Airways, which very soon had it in service on the Croydon to Paris route. Here it impressed with its reliability and the ability to operate in and out of a small intermediate airfield at Berck Mer on the north coast of France. Later in 1928, the Vanguard operated scheduled flights from London to Brussels and Cologne.

Once described as the world's largest passenger aircraft, the Vickers Vanguard. (Alamy)

In October 1928, it was withdrawn from scheduled flights for modifications to the tail assembly. It is believed that this involved the fitting of finless rudders, which had been successful on other Vickers aircraft, including the Victoria. On 16 May 1929, it took off on a test flight carrying a pilot and a test observer, but crashed at Shepperton in Middlesex, probably due to overstressing of the rear fuselage resulting in a catastrophic failure of the airframe. Both those on board were killed.

The sole Vanguard had a wingspan of 87ft 9in (26.75m) and its length was 53ft 10in (16.41m). With the Condor engines, it had a top speed of 112mph (180km/h).

The Air Ministry issued **Specification 34/24**, calling for a civilian mail- and freight-carrying aircraft. Vickers' response was a large biplane, metal-framed with fabric covering, and with balanced ailerons on both the lower and upper wings. This was the **Vickers Vellore** and behind the crew of two, seated side by side in an open cockpit, was the cargo compartment. The tail assembly was unusual; it was a biplane arrangement with four rudders, but no fins.

The first aircraft, the Vellore I, flew for the first time on 17 May 1928, fitted with a single Bristol Jupiter IX engine delivering 515hp (384kW). Demonstrated at RAF Hendon and tested at RAF Martlesham Heath, the Vellore performed very well and, given its size, better than expected. Its wingspan was 78ft (23.16m) and it had a top speed of 114mph (183km/h).

The extremely large Vickers Vellore prototype, photographed in 1929. (Picryl)

In early 1929, it received a new engine, an Armstrong Siddeley Jaguar VI, and the freight compartment was fitted with additional fuel tanks. On 19 March, it departed from Lympne in Kent, bound for Australia. The journey took a number of stages, but when it reached Benghazi, Libya, the engine caused some trouble. Spares arrived and repairs were carried out, after which the flight continued, but over the Timor Sea between Indonesia and Australia, the engine again malfunctioned. A forced landing occurred on the north coast of Australia, in a sparsely populated area; the Vellore was wrecked by contact with a tree.

Vickers did not pursue development of the single-engine Vellore. Instead, it embarked on a twin-engine development powered by two Bristol Jupiter XIF engines each producing 525hp (391kW). These were mounted in cowlings with Townend rings midway between the wings. Strangely, this aircraft was called the **Vickers Vellore III**, although there had not been a Vellore II. Like its single-engine predecessor, it was a mail/cargo aircraft and was designed so that it could be converted to a float plane. Another example of this aircraft was built, differing only in having Bristol Jupiter IX engines with slightly higher compression. This was used until 1935, ferrying troops and military stores.

The sole Vickers Vellore III first flew in June 1930 and competed in the 1930 King's Cup Air Race in July. (Picryl)

A third airframe, which had not been completed, was developed as a ten-passenger airliner with large cargo loading doors on the starboard side, located at the wing trailing edge; it was called the **Vickers Type 212 Vellox**. There was a new, wider fuselage, an enclosed cockpit for the crew and windows in the passenger cabin. Power was provided by two Bristol Pegasus IM3 engines, each delivering 600hp (447kW). Its first flight was on 23 January 1934.

Vickers had high expectations for the Vellox, but the reality was that the sole example was acquired by Imperial Airways as a cargo/mail plane. In August 1936, it took off from Croydon but suffered a loss of power and crashed; the crew of two pilots and two wireless operators were killed.

In 1922, Vickers had employed a French aircraft designer called Michel H. M. J. Wibault as a consulting engineer. He was a strong advocate of metal construction for aircraft and had patented a method that used simple metal shapes to build the airframe, which was then covered with very thin corrugated light alloy sheets. These were riveted to each other and to the underlying framework. No machining was required and the skins on the wings were not under stress. Wibault had closely followed design methods adopted by Hugo Junkers and Claude Dornier in Germany.

The third Vickers design to adopt Wibault's construction methods was a ten-passenger commercial aircraft that could operate from poor quality airfields and therefore be suitable for countries with remote operations. The result was the **Vickers Viastra**, six of which were built, but each varied in terms of the number of engines installed and the passenger capacity. The Viastra had a square section fuselage and a biplane tail unit.

The first, the Type 160 Viastra, had three Armstrong Siddeley Lynx engines of 270hp (200kW) and had its first flight on 1 October 1930. It was later modified to carry two Bristol Jaguar engines, but then converted back to three engines. With each modification, its 'Type' number was changed.

The second and third Viastras built were 12-passenger aircraft of Type 198 for West Australian Airways. From March 1931, these aircraft flew the Perth to Adelaide route. Although one was lost in a landing accident in 1933, the other continued in operational service until 1936. These were twin-engine aircraft with Bristol Jupiter engines.

The last Vickers Viastra, G-ACCC, built for the Prince of Wales. (Nico Braas, 1001 Aircraftphotos.com)

A single-engine freighter version was built but not delivered and therefore never used. The most interesting version was the Type 259 Viastra X. This was a special aircraft built for the Prince of Wales (the future King Edward VIII). It was powered by two Bristol Pegasus radial engines and had seating for a party of seven. It was, as expected, a lavishly equipped aircraft with an under-body pannier for luggage. It also sported a spatted undercarriage, heating, blind-flying equipment and an autopilot. It first took to the air in April 1933, but it is not known to what extent His Royal Highness made use of the aircraft. It was retired at some point during 1937.

The Viastra II as used by West Australian Airways had a wingspan of 70ft (21.34m) and a length of 45 6in (13.87m). The twin Bristol Jupiter XIF engines, each of 525hp (391kW), gave the aircraft a top speed of 120mph (190km/h) and a range of 535 miles (861km).

In 1932, the Air Ministry issued Specification B.9/32 for a twin-engine day bomber with a particular requirement for high performance. A number of companies responded, including Vickers, and several designs were accepted by the Air Ministry, including the Vickers offering, which became the Vickers Wellington. The aircraft structure was most unusual, employing a geodetic system designed by Barnes Wallis, who is perhaps best known for his 'bouncing bomb' used on the May 1943 Dambusters Raid.

During 1944, it became apparent that World War Two was approaching its conclusion and thoughts were turning to transport needs when peace returned. Air Ministry Specification 17/44 called for an interim short/medium haul passenger aircraft. The reasoning behind the word 'interim' was that the new designs anticipated from the Brabazon Committee's requirements would take time to materialise.

Specifically, the Ministry of Aircraft Production placed an order for three prototype 'Wellington Transport Aircraft' to meet the Air Ministry's expectations. There was logic in this; the Wellington had proved itself to be a robust and reliable bomber and was the only such aircraft that had been produced throughout the duration of the war. In that sense, it was still 'current', with nearly 11,500 having been built.

Vickers sensibly speeded up the development of the required prototypes by using some of the well-tried Wellington components, in particular the wing and undercarriage, coupled to a new fuselage. The name on the Ministry contract was dropped and the new aircraft was called the **Vickers VC.1 Viking**.

The first prototype had its maiden flight on 22 June 1945, but on 23 April 1946, it crashed as a result of double engine failure. Fortunately, there were no fatalities. Trials of the prototypes continued and the Ministry of Aircraft Production placed an order for 50 production Vikings. The first of these flew on 23 March 1946 and was delivered to BOAC at Hurn Airport near Bournemouth on 20 April.

Meanwhile, the prototypes were evaluated by the RAF, which resulted in orders being placed for a military transport version called the Vickers Valetta and eventually to a navigation/bomber training version called the Vickers Varsity. Unlike the Viking and Valetta, the Varsity had a tricycle undercarriage.

A Vickers VC.1 Viking of British European Airways. (Johan Visschedijk, 1000Aircraftphotos.com)

The first 19 production Vikings had a flight crew of three, a stewardess and seating for 21 passengers. The fuselage was built of metal, as were the wings inboard of the engines. The outer wings were fabric-covered geodetic structures, as were the tail units. Feedback from operators meant that the next 14 aircraft were built with stressed-metal wings and tail units.

A change took place for the next 115 aircraft. These were built with the fuselage extended by 28in (71cm), allowing passenger capacity to be increased to 24. The engines fitted to all the production Vikings were Bristol Hercules of 1,690hp (1,261kW).

An interesting one-off development saw a production aircraft fitted with two Rolls-Royce Nene turbojets, and in this form it had its first flight on 6 April 1948. 25 July of that year marked the 39th anniversary of Louis Bleriot's crossing of the Channel, so the Nene-Viking flew from London Heathrow to Paris carrying letters to Bleriot's widow and son. The 222-mile (357km) flight took just 34 minutes, in which a top speed of 415mph (668km/h) was reached, and averaged 394mph (634km/h). In 1954, this aircraft was acquired by Eagle Aviation and converted to Bristol Hercules 634 piston engines before joining the fleet.

When production ceased in 1948, a total of 163 Vikings had been built. This number included 16 built for the RAF, four of which were for the King's Flight. British European Airways (BEA) adapted some to accommodate 38 passengers.

The first nine Vikings delivered to BOAC were transferred to BEA when that company was formed on 1 August 1946. BEA began its first scheduled Viking flights on 1 September of that year, flying from Northolt in London to Copenhagen, and went on to become a major user of the Viking on its European and UK routes, operating the aircraft for eight years. In 1951, BEA modified its remaining Viking fleet to accommodate 36 passengers as the Admiral Class. In 1954, BEA replaced the Vikings with more modern airliners with pressurised cabins.

When BEA sold its aircraft, numerous British and European independent airlines acquired them. Civilian operators of the Vickers Viking included airlines in Argentina, Austria, Belgium, Denmark, Egypt, France, Germany, India, Iraq, Kuwait, Mexico, Portugal, Pakistan, South Africa, Southern Rhodesia (now Zimbabwe), Switzerland, Trinidad and Tobago as well as many small UK airlines.

Given the air traffic control technologies of the early post-war era and the nature of airport approach and landing aids at the time, it is little wonder that accidents occurred. These were not, of course, limited to Europe or to the Vickers Viking. Even so, it is thought-provoking to realise that 56 of the 163 Vikings built were lost in accidents, one of which was a mid-air collision with a Soviet Yak-3 fighter near Berlin. There were six take-off or landing accidents, plus two disasters when the aircraft flew into mountains.

In overall judgement, although it may have begun life as a stop-gap airliner, the Vickers Viking played a key role in establishing post-war air routes, especially in Europe.

With Bristol Hercules 634 radial engines of 1,690hp (1,260kW) each, the Viking had a top speed of 263mph (423km/h) and a range of 1,700 miles (2,700km). Its wingspan was 89ft 3in (27.20m) and its length 65ft 2in (19.86m).

In 1960, Vickers (Aviation) Ltd was merged with Bristol, English Electric and Hunting Aircraft to form British Aircraft Corporation.

Chapter 17

Westland

Westland Aircraft Works was established as a division of Petters Ltd in 1915. Petters had been manufacturing stationary petrol and diesel engines for agricultural purposes since 1896, but founded the aircraft company to meet government requirements for construction under licence of aircraft during the Great War. The company's initial order was for 12 Short Type 184 floatplanes, but other orders followed.

Experience in aircraft construction prompted the company to design its own aircraft, but the military prototypes built during the Great War were not successful, primarily because of the unreliability of the ABC Wasp and ABC Dragonfly engines installed.

After the war, Westland recognised the potential for expansion of aviation into civil use and designed a light biplane transport aircraft that would carry three passengers in addition to the pilot. The aircraft was called the **Westland Limousine**, and was powered by a single Rolls-Royce Falcon III engine delivering 275hp (205kW). The passengers sat in an enclosed cabin and the pilot sat in the rear of this cabin, on the port side. His seat was set 30in (76cm) above the passengers and his head protruded above the cabin roof through a hole. This Limousine had its maiden flight in July 1919.

A second aircraft, designated Limousine II, followed in October 1919. These first two aircraft operated an experimental air mail service between Croydon and Le Bourget, Paris, for two months, beginning in September 1920.

The third Limousine was initially fitted with a new Cosmos Jupiter engine, but this was later replaced with a Rolls-Royce Falcon III. A further four aircraft were built and used by Instone Air Line on services between London, Paris and Brussels.

Westland Limousine G-EARV had an exciting life including seal and fishery spotting and involvement in a gold rush at Stag Bay in Labrador. (Picryl)

In 1920, the Air Ministry sponsored a Commercial Aircraft Competition. Westland designers and engineers decided to enter with a larger variant of the Limousine, designated the Limousine III. With a longer fuselage, greater wingspan and a redesigned tail unit, it was powered by a 450hp (336kW) Napier Lion II engine and could carry five passengers.

The rules of the competition, which took place in August, placed emphasis on short field landings, so wheel brakes were fitted. Competitors were required to clear a 50ft (15.24m) obstacle and stop within a circle marked on the ground. Side-slip landings were not permitted. Looking very smart with silver wings and an eau-de-Nil fuselage, the Limousine won the first prize in the small commercial aircraft category, Westland receiving a sum believed to be £7,500. One more Limousine III was built and was operated by Instone Air Line.

The first Limousine II and two of the Limousine II aircraft were sold in Newfoundland and used by the Aerial Survey Company (Newfoundland) Ltd. They were used until late 1923, carrying mail and passengers to remote locations. The original Limousine survived until 1925, when it was destroyed in a collision on the ground with a Fairey Fawn light bomber.

The Limousine III had a top speed of 118mph (190km/h) and a range of 520 miles (840km). The wingspan was 54ft (16.46m) and the length was 33ft 6in (10.21m).

Westland will always be remembered for the Lysander, used so successfully during World War Two. Post-war, the company had success with the Wyvern naval fighter, but is best known for helicopters. Between 1959 and 1961, the British government consolidated the UK's aircraft industry into three groups, and Westland was merged with the helicopter divisions of other companies, to form Westland Helicopters.

Time and Space

The years covered by this book saw many changes in technology, available engine power, knowledge and materials, which individually and collectively powered the pace and nature of commercial aircraft design. Just as important, growth in the desire and need for air transport, both for goods and people, fuelled demand and influenced the nature of the aircraft developed to meet the changing market.

These changes could be mapped in many ways, but the table below shows the change in passenger capacity over the decades.

Year of first flight (see note 1)	Aircraft	Passengers (see note 2)
1919	Handley Page W series	12
	Vickers Vimy Commercial	10
	Vickers Type 54 Viking	4
	Westland Limousine	3
1920	De Havilland DH.18	8
1921	Bristol Type 62 Ten-Seater	9
1922	Bristol Brandon	8
	De Havilland DH.34	9
	Vickers Vulcan	6–8
1923	De Havilland DH.50	4
	Supermarine Sea Eagle	6
	Vickers Vanguard	23
1924	Avro 561 Andover	12
1926	Armstrong Whitworth Argosy	20
	De Havilland DH.66 Hercules	7
1928	Short S.8 Calcutta	15
	Vickers Type 212 Vellore	Freight
1929	Avro 618 Ten	8
	Avro 619 Five	4
1930	Handley Page HP.42	24
	Handley Page HP.45	24
	Saunders-Roe A.19 Cloud	8
	Saunders-Roe A.21 Windhover	4–6
	Vickers Viastra	12
1932	Airspeed AS.4 Ferry	10
	De Havilland DH.84 Dragon	10
	De Havilland DH.83 Fox Moth	3–4
	Spartan Cruiser	6
1933	Short S.16 Scion	6
1934	Airspeed A.6 Envoy	8
	Avro 642 Eighteen	16

Year of first flight (see note 1)	Aircraft	Passengers (see note 2)
1934 (*Cont.*)	De Havilland DH.86 Express	10–12
	De Havilland DH.89 Dragon Rapide	8
	Short L.17 Scylla	39
	Vickers Type 313 Vellox	10
1935	Avro 652	4
	Blackburn H.S.T.10	12
1936	Short S23 Empire	17
	Miles M.8 Peregrine	6
1937	De Havilland DH.91 Albatross	22
	Percival Q.6 Petrel	6
	Short S20 Mercury	Mail
	Short S21 Maia	18
1938	Armstrong Whitworth Ensign	40
	De Havilland DH.95 Flamingo	17
1939	Short S26	12–24
1942	Avro York	21
	Short Hythe	22
1943	Avro 691 Lancastrian	9
	Handley Page HP.70 Halton	10
1945	Avro 688 Tudor I	12
	Bristol Type 170 Freighter and Wayfarer	20
	De Havilland DH.104 Dove	8–11
	Miles Aerovan	10
	Miles M.65 Gemini	4
	Short S25 Sandringham	22
	Vickers Viking VC.1	21
1946	Airspeed AS.65 Consul	8
	Avro 689 Tudor II	60
	Handley Page HPR 1 Marathon	20
	Short S45A Solent	24–36
1947	Airspeed Ambassador	47
	Handley Page HP.81 Hermes	40–82
	Percival P.47 Mesanger	5–6
1948	Percival Prince	8
1949	Bristol Type 167 Brabazon	100 (see note 3)
1950	De Havilland DH.114 Heron	14–17
1955	Handley Page HPR 3 Herald	44
	Scottish Aviation Twin Pioneer	16
1965	Britten-Norman BN-2 Islander	9
1970	Britten-Norman Trislander	17

Note 1: The year of an aircraft's first flight does not necessarily indicate when it entered operational service.

Note 2: The number of possible passenger seats can vary greatly as an airline configures its aircraft for specific routes and passenger densities.

Note 3: Includes 23 seated in rear-facing cinema.

Other books you might like:

Historical Commercial
Aircraft Series,
Vol. 16

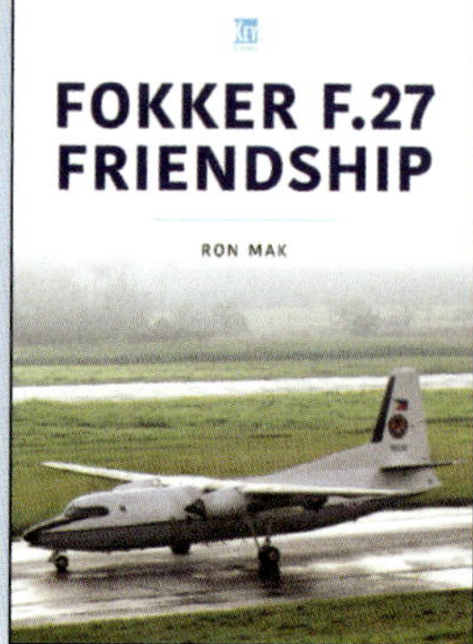

Historical Commercial
Aircraft Series,
Vol. 17

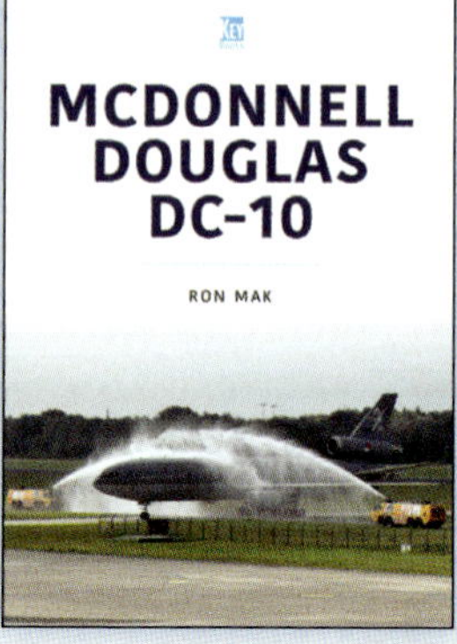

Historical Commercial
Aircraft Series,
Vol. 18

Historical Commercial
Aircraft Series,
Vol. 19

Historical Commercial
Aircraft Series,
Vol. 20

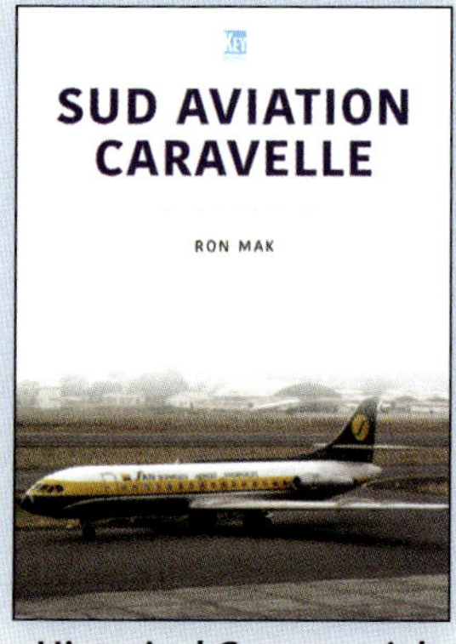

Historical Commercial
Aircraft Series,
Vol. 23

For our full range of titles please visit:
shop.keypublishing.com/books

VIP Book Club

Sign up today and receive
TWO FREE E-BOOKS

Be the first to find out about our forthcoming
book releases and receive exclusive offers.

Register now at **keypublishing.com/vip-book-club**

*Our VIP Book Club is a 100% spam-free zone, and we will never share your email with anyone else.
You can read our full privacy policy at: privacy.keypublishing.com*